THE SEVEN CHURCHES OF ASIA

KNOW YOUR BIBLE SERIES

••••••••••••••••••••

A STUDY COURSE OF
THE SEVEN CHURCHES
OF ASIA

••••••••••••••••••••

White Wing Publishing House and Press
Cleveland, Tennessee U.S.A. and Other Nations

ACD
31696

The Seven Churches of Asia
Copyright ©2002
Published by White Wing Publishing House
P.O. Box 3000 • Cleveland, Tennessee, U.S.A. 37320-3000
(423) 559-5425 • 1-800-221-5027
http://www.wingnet.net
All rights reserved
Cover art: Sixto Ramírez
Reprint 2002

ISBN # 1-889505-38-2

CONTENTS

Important Instructions 3
Lesson One
A Preview of the Course 5
Lesson Two
The Relationship of the Seven Churches to
the Overall Revelation 12
Lesson Three
The Church at Ephesus 20
Lesson Four
The Church at Smyrna 40
Lesson Five
The Church at Pergamos 56
Lesson Six
The Church at Thyatira 73
Lesson Seven
The Church at Sardis 88
Lesson Eight
The Church at Philadelphia 105
Lesson Nine
The Church at Laodicea 119
Lesson Ten
Postview and Summation 138

Examination 145

—Lesson One—

A PREVIEW OF THE COURSE

THE GEOGRAPHICAL, CULTURAL, AND HISTORICAL SITUATION

The "seven churches of Asia" under study in the course before us are named in Revelation 1:11. The use of a good Bible Atlas and a map in a recent edition of a World Atlas or Encyclopedia will be helpful at this point, and again as we take up the study of each church.

Baker's Bible Atlas describes Asia Minor as "a peninsula in western Asia ... bounded on the north by the Black Sea, on the south by the Mediterranean, and on the west by the Aegean arm of the Mediterranean." Today it is part of the Turkish Republic known as Anatolia, which means "the sunrise." The peninsula juts westward to within a mile of Europe at the northwest, across either of two straits—the Dardenelles or the Bosporus.

In John's day these seven cities were located in a province of Asia Minor known as "Asia"—thus "the seven churches which are in Asia." The "isle that is called Patmos" (1:10), where John was exiled, and where he wrote the Book of Revelation, was a small, bleak, mountainous isle (about 50 square miles in area) of the Sporades group of islands in the Aegean Sea. It was located about seventy miles southwest of Ephesus, and south of the Island of Samos.

Each of the lessons in this course begins with a brief account of the geographical and cultural situation, and some historical data concerning the particular city and church under study. The main body of the course pertains to the contents of the biblical record in chapters one through three.

INTRODUCING THE REVELATION OF JESUS CHRIST

The full and proper title of the Bible book from which this study course is taken is the first five words of that book ... "The Revelation of Jesus Christ" (Revelation 1:1). John modestly mentions himself (verses 1 and 4) merely as the scribe, as it were, who recorded that which a God-sent angel bade him write (1:1):

> "The Revelation of Jesus Christ, which God gave unto him [Jesus Christ], to shew unto his servants things

which must shortly come to pass; and he [Jesus Christ] sent and signified it by his angel unto his servant John."

Despite John's modesty, he is designated as Christ's "servant"—an honorable title for any man! On the one hand, John was bidden to "write" in his own words the overall description of what he had just presently seen, what he was presently seeing and hearing, and what he would soon be shown concerning the future (1:11, 19). On the other hand, he was commanded to "write" the exact words given him, as by dictation, the messages to the seven churches of Asia (e.g. 2:1). The words of the entire book, or revelation, are either directly or indirectly the words of Christ, for John was "in the Spirit on the Lord's day" (1:10) when the command came from "Alpha and Omega" (Christ) to write. Doubtless John was "in the Spirit" as each segment of the total revelation came before his view, and was moved by the Holy Ghost to make the record as Christ "signified it by his angel unto his servant John" (1:1).

The word "revelation," as used here and in Scripture generally, means more than simply coming to know or understand something through the normal development of the mental processes; e.g., adult comprehension as opposed to that of a young child. Here, "revelation" is the translation of **apokalypsis,** which means: A disclosure, discovery, or uncovering of that which had previously been covered or hidden; an unveiling.

It is important to understand that the full revelation—the entire book of twenty-two chapters—is addressed to the churches (1:4, 11). Since the book is prophecy more than it is history, it seems clear that its message is intended for the Church of God from John's day until now, and on unto the ultimate consummation of the vision. This being the case, our study of the Church's role relative to that which is written should be pursued prayerfully and soberly.

JOHN'S PERSONAL SALUTATION AND EXPLANATION

The Salutation

John identifies himself as the writer; then he addresses "the seven churches which are in Asia" as the recipients. He explains that the "grace" and "peace" which he extends is: (1) from God—"him which IS, and which WAS, and which IS TO COME"; (2) "from the SEVEN SPIRITS which are before the throne"; and (3) "from JESUS CHRIST, who is the faithful witness, and the first begotten of the dead, and the prince of the kings of the earth" (1:4, 5).

Reference to "the seven Spirits" is understood by some as ministering angels, citing Revelation 3:1, 4:5, and 5:6 as "proof." However, the capitalization of "Spirits"—if warranted—would hardly be used of angels. Others favor the Holy Ghost, sevenfold in His operations, or attributes. They cite Isaiah 11:2 and 1 Corinthians 12:4-7. It may be noteworthy, considering the context of the salutation (1:4), that both God and Christ are mentioned along with "the seven Spirits." It seems possible, at least, that the Holy Ghost is intended as completing the Holy Trinity. However, ministering angels appear throughout the revelation. (See 1:1, 5:2; 7:1, 2; 8:2; 10:1; 14:6; 15:1; 16:1; 18:1; 19:17; 20:1, 2; 21:9; 22:8; and 22:16 with 1:1.) The subject is treated more fully in Lesson Seven of this course.

In a spirit of praise, John, who was an eyewitness of the crucifixion of his beloved Master and Lord, attributes "glory and dominion for ever and ever" to Him who so loved poor, sinful men that He shed His precious blood to "wash[ed] us from our sins" (1:5, 6). He gave His life for ours! Yes, GLORY and DOMINION to the One who loves like this! Hallelujah!

Still in a ecstasy of praise, John speaks of Christ's second coming (1:7), when with "glory and dominion" He will set up His millennial kingdom. It is at that second phase of His second coming that He will come with clouds (Mark 14:62; Matthew 24:30), and all will see Him (Matthew 24:27), including those who pierced Him and rejected Him, and will mourn and wail when at last they see their awful sin of unbelief (Matthew 24:30; Zechariah 12:10).

Verse eight is a mighty benediction to the salutation, in words given to John in the first person, and quoted by John—"I am Alpha and Omega, the beginning and the ending..." (saith the Lord). The words are a confirmation of what John had already said.

The Explanation to the Churches

The saints in the local churches to whom he was writing

were well acquainted with the aged Apostle John. He was indeed their "brother." They knew the tribulations he had suffered and endured, and he knew theirs (1:9). John was still experiencing the tribulation of exile on Patmos for preaching the Word of God and giving testimony concerning Jesus Christ.

In verses ten through twenty, John details his awesome confrontation with the glorified Christ and the imperative commission—

". . . What thou seest, write in a book, and send it unto the seven churches which are in Asia; unto Ephesus, and unto Smyrna, and unto Pergamos, and unto Thyatira, and unto Sardis, and unto Philadelphia, and unto Laodicea" (1:11).

The fact that John was "in the Spirit" (1:10), along with the nature of what he saw when he "turned to see the voice" that had spoken, makes it clear that he was under an extraordinary spiritual influence. The "isle called Patmos" had faded from his view and he was seeing other scenes through the spiritual eye. The expressions of different commentators are interesting:

The Pulpit Commentary paraphrases John's words this way: "I came to be in a state of ecstasy capable of receiving revelations."

Greek Expositor **Kenneth S. Wuest** says: "I entered into a different experience in the sphere of the Spirit [His absolute control] . . . ."

Commentator **John F. Walvoord,** in his "The Revelation of Jesus Christ," says: "John's statement . . . refers to his experience of being beyond normal sense into a state where God could reveal supernaturally the contents of this book."

Matthew Henry expresses John's experience as follows: "He was not only in a rapture when he received the vision, but before he received it; he was in a serious, heavenly, spiritual frame, under the blessed, gracious influence of the Spirit of God."

Adam Clarke says it somewhat differently: "I received the Spirit of prophecy, and was under its influence when the first vision was exhibited."

Some thirty years before John's experience, the Apostle

Paul had explained in simple terms how God had gotten His Word on record:

> "... No prophecy of the scripture is of any private interpretation.
>
> "For the prophecy came not in old time by the will of man: but holy men of God spake as they were moved by the Holy Ghost" (2 Peter 1:20, 21).

And God had not changed His manner and method in John's day—nor Peter's—nor Paul's. The "move" may have varied slightly, but the agency was always "by the Holy Ghost." We are convinced, therefore, that the record before us was made by the supernatural anointing of God upon His "servant John" (1:1). This being true, along with the fact that it is a **revelation** and not a hidden **mystery,** it follows that this message to the churches bears a relevance for our day that must not be taken lightly.

CHRIST'S MANY MESSAGES
Among the first things to which new Christians are introduced is Christ's famous "Sermon on the Mount"—His longest on record. Later they learn of numerous other distinctive discourses. A few examples include (1) The mysteries of the kingdom, in Matthew 13; (2) exhortation to humble servanthood, in Matthew 18, Mark 9, and Luke 9; (3) the law of forgiveness, in Matthew 18 and Luke 17; (4) the rebuke of hypocrisy, in Matthew 23 and Mark 7; (5) the signs of the times, in Matthew 24 and Luke 21; (6) divorce and remarriage, in Matthew 19 and Mark 10; (7) the new birth, in John 3; (8) the bread of life, in John 6; (9) the truth and the light, in John 8; (10) the one Shepherd and His fold, in John 10; and (11) the indwelling Holy Ghost, in John 14, 15, and 16.

Then consider all the "sermonettes" incidental to His everyday ministry, sometimes in parables, and always by His authority as the Son of the Father.

All of His teachings were wonderful, and they remain so. But the observation of **John F. Walvoord** concerning Revelation, chapters two and three, is all too true. He says:

> "It is remarkable that so little attention has been paid to the importance of these two chapters...."

"... Many casual worshippers in Christian churches today who are quite familiar with the **Sermon on the Mount** are not aware of the existence of these seven messages of Christ. Their **incisive character** and **pointed denunciation** of departure from biblical morality and theology have tended to keep them out of the mainstream of contemporary theological thought. Many of the evils and shortcomings which exist in the church today are a direct outgrowth of neglect of the solemn instruction given to these seven churches."

In this study course, we will face up to the "incisive character and pointed denunciation" of these messages, despite the bane being touted today against "negativism." We will point out the "positivism" also, endeavoring to remember that our God of love is no respecter of persons. He is LOVE when He says "DON'T" and "THOU SHALT NOT," the same as when He says "DO" and "THOU SHALT."

The whole revelation deals with "things which must shortly come to pass" (1:1). In light of the fact that much, if not most, of the book's contents is yet to be fulfilled after almost two millenniums since John's day, what does this statement mean? As used here, the word "shortly" (**entachei**) means that, in God's own time, the "things" mentioned will quickly or suddenly be done in rapid succession, once their fulfillment has begun. A similar word (**tachys**) is translated "quickly" seven times in Revelation (2:15, 16; 3:11; 11:14; 22:7, 12, 20).

Generally, the "short work" of Romans 9:28 carries the same meaning. It was a long time between God's promise of redemption (Genesis 3:15) and the finished work on Calvary (John 19:30), but once God had begun the vital part of the fulfillment, it was finished in approximately three and a half years. Similarly, once God begins fulfilling this "revelation," He will rapidly carry it to its conclusion. It is not impossible that these "things" might now be in the process of quickly and rapidly coming to pass!

As with many of the Old Testament prophecies, this revelation probably entails a two-fold fulfillment: **First**, pertaining to the tribulations inflicted on Christians by the Roman authorities in the early centuries, which are confirmed by history; and **second,** a more pertinent application for the time of the Antichrist tribulation period, and on to the glorious eternity of the new heaven and the new earth.

—Lesson Two—

THE RELATIONSHIP OF THE SEVEN CHURCHES TO THE OVERALL REVELATION

RELEVANCE OF FUTURE PROPHECY TO EXTANT CHURCHES

Although the specific purpose of this course is to examine the messages, or letters, to seven particular local churches, certainly they have a pertinent relationship to the whole revelation. This is borne out by the fact that these personal letters appear immediately following the introductory passages. Since the revelation pertains to future events, most of which will transpire after the rapture of the Church, why the letters to currently existing local bodies?

The early presentation of the letters seems an invitation, or admonition, for those churches to ponder their present condition in relation to their **responsibility** and **accountability** in the light of future end-results. After all, in the end, whether "the time is at hand" (Revelation 1:3) or "at the time of the end" (Daniel 12:9), "... every one of us shall give account of himself to God" (Romans 14:12—every member of every local church, every believer, and every unbeliever).

So, in God's eyes, how were these seven churches doing at the time they received the letters? If they should continue their present course, would they stand approved or condemned in the end? If they were presently displeasing to God, just what were His expectations for them henceforward? All things considered, would they render the response so clearly expected of them? In the end, would their candlesticks be removed, or would they remain?

Why These Particular Churches? Conjecture is all we have with which to answer this question. Some suggestions that have been set forth include: (1) John possibly had the oversight of these seven churches. He was now an aged man, and this "crescent" of local churches would have been convenient for him to oversee. (2) Each of the seven may have been in some way normative, illustrating conditions common to local congregations at that time, as well as in every age, including our own. Whether or not it was His particular design to speak to all local churches, or to the Church in general, through the ages, we must confess that it would be difficult to think of anything relative to the churches today that He has not already treated in these seven letters. (3) The number seven may have been used symbolically of them all, and in some sense may have suggested perfection. (4) A less likely one, especially in light of the Church of God of Prophecy's revelation of the Church, suggests that the contents of the letters indicate a chronological development of Church history spiritually. This would necessarily mean that the Church would regress spiritually rather than going on to perfection. The condition of the church at Laodicea would have to represent a final apostasy rather than a glorious Church without spot, blemish, or wrinkle which Christ will present unto Himself (Ephesians 5:26, 27). **A. J. Tomlinson's** position, and that of the Church, has been that the prophetic apostasy, or falling away (2 Thessalonians 2:3) took place following the Council at Nicea in A.D. 325, when the Dark Ages began. This period ended on June 13, 1903 when the Church returned to "Arise, shine" until Jesus comes.

The "religious conglomerate" of our day truly suggests an apostasy. Many are shouting "Lord! Lord!" and professing all kinds of "wonderful works" IN HIS NAME (Matthew 7:21-23). But, rightly dividing the Word of truth (2 Timothy 2:15), this apostate spectacle of deception is not the Church of the living God.

Apparently, we must leave the reason for the selection of "the seven churches which are in Asia" to Jesus Christ, who told John what to write, and where to send the writings when finished. Since God is no respecter of persons, we may safely say that everything that was said to, and about, those churches He is still saying to whomsoever it applies in the Church in these last days.

Expositor **John F. Walvoord** gives the following preview of chapters two and three, as to their setting in the revelation:

> "... Chapter 1 seems to fulfill the command of 1:19, 'Write the things which thou HAST SEEN' [in verses 10 through 18]. Beginning in chapter 4, the material deals with 'the things which SHALL BE HEREAFTER' (1:19). In chapters 2 and 3, the messages to the seven churches are referred to as 'the things which ARE' (cf 1:19). These

messages [to the churches] therefore, contain divine revelation and exhortation pertaining to the [then] present age; and, having special pertinence in the present situation in the church, they [chapters 2 and 3] constitute one of the most incisive [sharp, keen, piercing] and penetrating exhortations in the entire New Testament in relation to church doctrine and Christian living."

JOHN'S RESPONSE TO HIS ASSIGNMENT

The Voice and the Candlesticks

It is evident that John was overwhelmed to the point of falling at the feet of Christ as dead (1:17). First, he had heard the voice (1:10) "as the sound of many waters" (1:15), which had, in only a few words, identified the Speaker and had given the unexpected assignment (1:10, 11). The churches (candlesticks) are prominent in the very beginning of the vision. John saw them first, when he turned "to see the voice" (1:12).

The Man in the Midst

Immediately after seeing the churches as candlesticks, John saw "one like unto the Son of man." Undoubtedly he knew at once it could be none other than Jesus. He was in the midst of the churches. This should not be surprising when we remember His promise to the Church even before He had purchased it with His own blood. Later, after all was made clear, perhaps John recalled His Master's words on one occasion:

"For where two or three are gathered together in my name, there am I in the midst of them" (Matthew 18:20).

"... Lo, I am with you alway, even unto the end of the world. Amen" (Matthew 28:20).

Now, to John He appears in all His awesome majesty and glory (1:13-16)—a vision similar to Daniel's. (Read Daniel 7:9-14.) Everything about Him spoke of godly power and authority:

(1) The "garment down to the foot" portrayed Him as both High Priest and Judge.

(2) The "golden girdle" spoke of priesthood and kingship.

(3) His "hairs... white like wool, as white as snow" denoted heavenly glory and purity, and possibly related to Daniel's reference to the "Ancient of days" (Daniel 7:9)—the Father's glory made visible in the Son.

(4) The "eyes... as a flame of fire" remind us of Solomon's words: "The eyes of the Lord are in every place, beholding the evil and the good" (Proverbs 15:3); also the seer Hanani's rebuke of Judah's king Asa: "For the eyes of the Lord run to and fro throughout the whole earth..." (2 Chronicles 16:9); see also Zechariah 4:10 with 3:9). **Walvoord** comments—"His eyes as a flame of fire speak of the searching righteousness and divine judgment upon all that is impure."

(5) "His feet like unto fine brass, as if they burned in a furnace," according to **Walvoord,** "symbolizes divine judgment as embodied in the Old Testament types of the brazen altar... Christ standing in the midst of the churches on the basis of divine and righteous judgment portrayed both in the fire and in the metal mentioned."

(6) "His voice as the sound of many waters" may indicate the divine Word that drowns out all other arguments, "revealing the majesty and power before which human authority must bow" (Walvoord).

(7) The "sharp twoedged sword" proceeding out of His mouth calls Hebrews 4:12 to mind: "For the word of God is quick [margin, **living** and **operative**], and powerful, and sharper than any two-edged sword, piercing even to the dividing asunder of the soul and spirit, and of the joints and marrow, and is a discerner of the thoughts and intents of the heart." It may also predict in advance the judgments about to be poured out upon this Christ-rejecting world, as are seen in chapters four through twenty.

(8) "His countenance [expression of the face] was as the sun shineth in his strength" depicts His heavenly glory and immediately agrees with that which John, along with Peter and James, had seen on the occasion of Christ's transfiguration, when "His face did shine as the sun" (Matthew 17:2) and "the fashion of his countenance was altered" (Luke 9:29); likewise, Paul's experience on the Damascus road, where "a light from heaven, above the brightness of the sun" (Acts 26:13) was part of his dramatic and humbling vision, at which he fell to the earth blind. And now, John falls at His feet as dead, in awesome dread and fear; but the living Lord soothingly says, "Fear not...."

THE MYSTERY INTERPRETED

After some blessed reassurances and a restatement of his assignment to "write," John was given an explanation directly related to his task. Until now, the meaning of the seven candlesticks and the seven stars had remained a mystery, but no longer:

> "The mystery of the seven stars which thou sawest in my right hand, and the seven golden candlesticks. The seven stars are the angels of the seven churches: and the seven candlesticks... are the seven churches" (Revelation 1:20).

The "angels" are generally considered to be the pastors of the churches. Some commentators use the word "messenger." The pastor bears God's message—the gospel and His Word generally—to the membership. Some have contended that each church has an angel, assigned by God, to watch over its affairs. But the question arises: How could John send a letter to an angel? He could write to the churches and their pastors, but hardly to an angel.

It should be an awesome thought to any pastor to learn that Christ holds him in His right hand. It is suggested that the seven stars grasped in Christ's hand indicates His power and purpose either to **defend them** or **dispose of them** at His will.

The churches as candlesticks indicates their responsibility as dispensers of the light of God's Word and will. Jesus portrayed the Church—in fact, each believer in it—as follows:

> "Ye are the light of the world. A city that is set on an hill cannot be hid.
>
> "Neither do men light a candle, and put it under a bushel, but on a candlestick; and it giveth light unto all that are in the house.
>
> "Let your light so shine before men, that they may see your good works, and glorify your Father which is in heaven" (Matthew 5:14-16).

The Church of God, through its many congregations, is on display before the world. All that is done, good or bad, is open to the view of all. The **responsibility** is momentous! The **accountability** is fearful!

It is little wonder, then, that the very first move of God in this great "revelation" should be that of calling the Church to account. It is His representative and His spokesman in this world, and it should be feverishly and relentlessly pursuing the commission that has been given to no other (Matthew 28:19, 20; Mark 16:15, 16). Even though it will be raptured before the major fulfillment of John's vision, there is a lost world to be evangelized and warned of the judgments that will befall those who refuse the gospel now.

Again, the Lord's Word to those early churches in Asia is not to be taken lightly by the Church today.

FOUR COMMON FEATURES IN ALL SEVEN LETTERS

In order to forego much space-consuming repetition, let us here consider four features common to all seven of the letters to the churches:

(1) Each letter begins with Christ's words to John as to the particular "angel," or pastor, to whom the message should be addressed.

We are not to be dogmatic in assuming that the full contents of the letter referred to the pastor, or to him only. It is more probable that he was simply the logical individual to receive the message, and that he was expected to read it to his congregation word-for-word.

Neither must we assume that nothing in the letter had reference to him. The pastor may rightly be called a church's "angel" in the sense of his role as guardian, guide, and protector of the flock. As such, he must himself be fit for the task. Furthermore, he is expected to administer spiritual nourishment kept free of any and all "foreign matter"—heresy and false doctrine. If any such is found in any member, it is the pastor's duty to deal with the matter until it is brought to the biblical conclusion. The very continuing existence of the church depends on its being kept pure.

Our unchanging God spoke to the pastors, shepherds, and prophets through Jeremiah and Ezekiel (Jeremiah 23; Ezekiel 34). They were charged with heavy responsibilities, and the judgments of God against their unfaithfulness were great. How much more should He expect of the New Testament Gospel-era pastor-shepherd who has been redeemed and sanctified by the blood of the Lamb, filled with the Holy Ghost, and called to be an ambassador for Christ!

(2) To each pastor and church Christ says, "I know thy works." Greek Expositor **Kenneth S. Wuest** states it emphatically—"I know with absolute clearness your works." God does not have to speculate. Outward appearances mean nothing to Him unless they correspond perfectly with what He sees in the heart.

"Works" have more than one meaning. They may be good deeds, or labor expended in the spread of the gospel. On the other hand, and foremost, they are the fruits of righteous living, such as obedience, holiness, and true worship; or "the works of the flesh" (Galatians 5:19-21), the issues of an evil heart. The point is that GOD KNOWS, and His judgments are just.

(3) To each individual member who is an "overcomer" He makes a promise—"He [or him—personally] that overcometh." The church will be victorious if its members are overcomers. He does not promise an easy way, but a reward to those who persevere to the end. **Webster** defines "overcome" thus: "To get the better of in competition, or struggle; to conquer." The secret seems to lie in a firm, unwavering belief in Christ, for John says:

> "For whatsoever is born of God overcometh the world: and this is the victory that overcometh the world, even our faith.
> "Who is he that overcometh the world, but he that believeth that Jesus is the Son of God?" (1 John 5:4, 5).

Of course, this is more than an intellectual belief, such as even the devils have and tremble at (James 2:19, 20). James explains that a "head" belief is not faith. The devils know only too well that there is a God; and so do his millions of slaves. But overcoming belief is the kind that is proven by the resultant works of loving service; not works in order TO BE SAVED, but works of worshipful heart-appreciation because we ARE SAVED. This is the overcomer's solid rock!

(4) Each believer in each church is given an exhortation—"He that hath an ear, let him hear what the Spirit saith unto the churches." Christ demands **an immediate response** to what the Holy Ghost is saying in these letters—"He that hath ears, let him hear **at once** . . . ." Each one has the personal respon-

sibility to hear for himself. Even though his local church may perish, yet he shall live if he personally overcomes. On the other hand, his local church may be faithful, yet he will lose the reward if he is unfaithful.

Remember Jesus' very understandable explanation concerning the two houses, one built on a rock, the other on the sand. When the storm came, the outcome was determined by the words, "Whosoever HEARETH these sayings of mine, and DOETH THEM," or "DOETH THEM NOT" (Matthew 7:24-27). Some things are common to all, but each church and each member—then and now—must hear those things in particular that the Holy Ghost is ever trying to get us to hear and acknowledge. This shows the Lord's omniscience, and His care and concern for each church and each individual.

—Lesson Three—

THE CHURCH AT EPHESUS

RELATIONSHIP OF CITY AND CHURCH

The Geographical, Cultural, and Historical Situation

Geography: Ephesus was situated on the western coast of the Roman province of Asia, in the district of Lydia, near the mouth of the Cayster River. The population is thought to have been about three million. Ephesus ranked first among the cities of this Roman province, and was the capital city.

It was a terminal for caravan routes from Europe and the Orient. Today, the ruins of the old city are about five miles inland because of the silt deposit at the mouth of the river. According to the **Thompson Bible Survey,** "The modern seaport of Ephesus is now Kusadai, about twenty miles (southwest) from where the ancient city stood."

Culture and History: The history of Ephesus dates back to around 1044 B.C. when the ancient district of Ionia was colonized by the Greeks, the European country of Greece being just across the Aegean Sea to the west. It was under a number of other powers through the years, becoming a part of the Roman Empire about 133 B.C. It was an important trade and banking center, as well as the site of popular athletic events and pageantry.

Perhaps Ephesus is best remembered for its "religious" prosperity: (1) The oriental cult that worshipped Artemis, the Greek goddess of the moon, wild animals, and hunting **(Webster).** The Roman name for Artemis was Diana. The Temple of Diana was one of the ancient "Seven Wonders of the World." (2) A Christian center after its evangelization by Apostle Paul about A.D. 56, where he met the opposition of the worshippers of "Diana of the Ephesians" head-on. (Read Acts, chapter 19.) Paul had established the church there some forty years before John received the revelation on Patmos; and now it had been thirty-two years since he had written the **Epistle to the Ephesians.**

Sensual immorality was something of a "trade mark" in Ephesus, it being a legitimate part of most "eastern religions." But the coming of Christianity had interfered with this immoral, idolatrous lifestyle, and the diminishing returns from the sale of "silver shrines for Diana" had caused an uproar (Acts 19:40). Paul had stayed at Ephesus three years or more (Acts 20:31), and from the tone of his epistle to them perhaps two years after leaving there, the church was well established in the faith. Christ's letter, written by John's hand, fills us in on how they were doing still thirty years later.

CHRIST INTRODUCES HIMSELF

"Unto the angel of the church of Ephesus write; These things saith he that holdeth the seven stars in his right hand, who walketh in the midst of the seven golden candlesticks" (Revelation 2:1).

This church and its "angel," or pastor, was addressed first, possibly because John's residence in later years was at Ephesus. Jesus introduced Himself, first as "He that holdeth the seven stars in His right hand." This pastor was one of those stars. The word "hold," as used here, means "to hold authoritatively." The pastors were held not only in God's hand of **protection,** but also in His hand of **control.**

As Peter has said, ministers are not to be "lords." the people are God's heritage, and the pastors are to be ensamples to their flocks—compassionate, caring shepherds—feeding them and watching out for their spiritual welfare; all by the constraint of love, and not for money. (Read 1 Peter 5:1-4.)

Jesus' second identification of Himself was as He "who walketh in the midst of the seven golden candlesticks." He was not merely there; He was walking among them. His presence was comforting and reassuring, but His eternal vigilance and all-encompassing observation also made them aware that He saw their **shortcomings** as well as their **virtues.**

The believer who has a heart-desire to please the Lord need not dread His continual presence, but should rather be grateful for His ever-readiness to give nurture to his weakness and strength in times of temptation. However, His presence is a reminder of our responsibility and accountability.

Through these two identifications by way of introduction, both pastor and church were assured that, on Christ's part, there was solid ground for perfect trust.

CHRIST'S APPRAISAL OF THE CHURCH

"I know thy works, and thy labour, and thy patience, and how thou canst not bear them which are evil: and thou hast tried them which say they are apostles, and are not, and hast found them liars:
"And hast borne, and hast patience, and for my name's sake hast laboured, and hast not fainted" (Revelation 2:2, 3).

The positive, emphatic statement, **"I know thy works,"** is the basis for His righteous appraisal of the church; both of its **praiseworthiness** and its **blameworthiness**. Their works included the whole scope of their conduct—the labors and their behavior.

The Many Commendations

(1) **He knew their labors,** mentioning them twice, but in different aspects (verses 2 and 3). There was the manual, physical labor in various activities; but principally, that which was required in the interest of the spiritual welfare of the saints and the community. These labors were shared by the pastor and the church.

In verse three the context suggests a sort of labor resulting from things that were difficult and unpleasant; but they had expended this effort for Christ's name's sake. Considering the upcoming rebuke (verse 4), we must ask: **Is it possible to labor for Christ's name's sake without a love He can accept?** Apparently so, since Christ Himself says this church did it. The discussion under verse four below will examine this further. But now, as they heard this letter being read, they may have pondered **the true motives** they had had as they had labored. Perhaps other thoughts on the subject came to their minds, which Paul and others had said or written:

"Remembering without ceasing your work of faith, and labour of love, and patience of hope in our Lord Jesus Christ, in the sight of God our Father" (1 Thessalonians 1:3).

"For God is not unrighteous to forget your work and labour of love, which ye have shewed toward his name, in that ye have ministered to the saints, and do minister" (Hebrews 6:10).

"Now he that planteth and he that watereth are one: and every man shall receive his own reward according to his own labour" (1 Corinthians 3:8).

"Therefore, my beloved brethren, be ye stedfast, unmoveable, always abounding in the work of the Lord, forasmuch as ye know that your labour is not in vain in the Lord" (1 Corinthians 15:58).

Then in his Epistle to the Ephesians some thirty-two years earlier, Paul had admonished this same church:

"Let him that stole steal no more: but rather let him labour, working with his hands the thing which is good, that he may have to give to him that needeth" (Ephesians 4:28).

And there was the time when he had called the Ephesian elders to meet him at Miletus, where he exhorted them, and where they bade one another their last farewells. On that occasion Paul had said:

"I have coveted no man's silver, or gold, or apparel.
"Yea, ye yourselves know, that these hands have ministered unto my necessities, and to them that were with me.
"I have shewed you all things, how that so labouring ye ought to support the weak, and to remember the words of the Lord Jesus, how he said, It is more blessed to give than to receive" (Acts 20:33-35).

(2) **He knew their patience.** This too He mentioned twice: (a) Patience in labor (verse 2), and (b) patience in bearing long with wrongdoers (verse 3). They had patiently continued on, even in the face of persecution, discouragement, and the opposition they had had from the Jews, and also from the worshippers of Diana (Acts 19:23-41).

There is a "bearing patience" which God gives to endure the injuries and hurts that men inflict upon us, as well as the reproofs we deserve. Then there is a "waiting patience," that when we have done the will of God, we may wait on Him for the promise (Hebrews 10:36). Though there are times when there seems no alternative to bearing sufferings and reverses, it is commendable, as Jesus said, when we bear these things with patience.

In the context of verse two with verse three, the church at Ephesus had probably borne patiently the problem with the false apostles; but this did not preclude their responsibility to exercise the required discipline. One of the Christian's virtues is to be "patient in tribulation" (Romans 12:12). Paul says that we who are justified by faith "glory in tribulations also: knowing that tribulation worketh patience; and patience, experience; and experience, hope" (Romans 5:3, 4). However, Peter qualifies this somewhat by explaining that **the reason** for our suffering makes a difference: "For what glory is it, if, when ye be buffeted for your faults, ye take it patiently? but if, when ye do well, and suffer for it, ye take it patiently, this is acceptable with God" (1 Peter 2:20).

James explains that the trying of our faith works patience, and if we will let patience have its perfect work, it will produce perfection in us (James 1:3,4)

Then, there is the part which patience plays in the reward of eternal life: "Who [God] will render to every man according to his deeds: to them who by patient continuance in well-doing seek for glory and honour and immortality, [the reward is] eternal life" (Romans 2:6, 7).

The "dash" of a restless enthusiasm may be good under some circumstances, but more important is the attribute of a dogged persistence and a power to endure "over the long haul." There are many who start well in the Christian race, but the "prize-winner" is the one who crosses "the finish line" (1 Corinthians 9:24-27). To the Ephesian elders, Paul had expressed his determination to finish his course with joy (Acts 20:24).

In these perilous last days (2 Timothy 3:1), many fail to serve the Lord patiently. The tendency is to make compromises with both moral and theological evils rather than take a stand and wait with patience for the right to prevail.

(3) He knew their abhorrence of evil—" . . . thou canst not bear [tolerate; endure] them that are evil." Note two points here:

(a) There may be at least a marginal difference between

"ARE evil" and "DO evil." There are people who are so inherently evil, so given over to evil, that they are almost the personification of evil. They DO evil because they ARE evil. Apparently this was the element Jesus referred to. Others DO evil things only because of having been born with the depravity which all human beings have inherited by Adam's fall. It is not their unrestrained practice, but the unjustified, unsanctified nature gets the upper hand despite any struggle they might wage against it.

(b) There may also be a marginal difference between PERSONS who are evil and the EVIL itself. Any child of God should abhor evil itself as the chief attribute of their adversary, the devil. But usually we can bear (put up with) persons who do evil deeds short of having made themselves reprobates. The saints at Ephesus could not bear those reprobate persons because of the overwhelming predominance of evil in them.

These were not necessarily people who had crept into the church unawares, though that was at least a possibility (Jude 4; Acts 20:29). Some work from the outside to entice members away. We live in an evil world, of which Satan is the "prince" (John 12:21; Ephesians 2:2). Every church is situated in some city or community that is predominantly evil, or of this world system under Satan's power. Jesus prayed: "I pray not that thou [Father] shouldest take them out of the world, but that thou shouldest keep them from the evil. They are not of the world, even as I am not of the world" (John 17:15, 16). We are left here as ambassadors for Christ, to reconcile men and women to God (2 Corinthians 5:20). He has left the Church here as a light lifted up on a hill to glorify the Father which is in heaven (Matthew 5:14-16). This leaves no room for us to condone sin, nor to make any concessions whatsoever to men's evil ways.

We see all around us among professing Christians a weak-kneed tolerance for "giving in" to wickedness; a cowardliness in the face of Satan's defiant brazenness. We see also a boasted "broad-mindedness—camouflaged as love, or patience, or wisdom, or understanding, or empathy—all attributes that are good when used legitimately, not pretentiously. The real problem is (1) a lack of holy boldness for God and His righteousness; and (2) a dimming vision of the Christ of Calvary—His pierced side and His nail-scarred hands and feet—FOR US!

All such flimzy cowardice leads to compromise and deception. When looked squarely in the face, it is a betrayal of the Christ once again by selling out His gospel into the hands of those who delight in finding false witnesses against it. (Remember Judas—Luke 22:1-6, 47-53; Matthew 27:3-10?) it is also a denial that we know Him. (Remember Peter—Luke 22:54-62?)

In the spirit of love and forbearance, we must deal with wrongdoers as Jesus directed (Matthew 18:15-17); not with a cold, mechanical legalism, but a caring, compassionate desire to save or restore them. But there are those times when there is no just alternative to exclusion. This disciplinary process has three objectives: (a) **The glory of God,** in that it upholds His holiness; (b) **the purity of the Church,** in that it prevents "a little leaven [sin]" from defiling the whole lump [church membership]; and (c) **the spiritual good of the member who must be corrected,** in that he or she is not erroneously made to think that sin is inconsequential.

(4) **He knew they had tried the false apostles**—"thou hast tried them which say they are apostles, and are not, and hast found them liars." At the time of the "revelation," all the apostles were dead except John. Possibly there were numerous individuals with ulterior ambitions—visions of power and prestige by self-exaltation and political maneuvering—who hoped to take the place of the original twelve. Information is meager on the requirements for apostleship, but it seems clear that the original ones were not to be replaced.

The word "apostle" means: "One chosen and sent with a special commission as the fully authorized representative of the sender." Since Jesus was the Commissioner, or Sender, it has been the consensus of Bible expositors through the centuries that He alone had the authority to select apostles. As to the requirements, some conclusions have been offered, as follows: (a) All must have seen and known Jesus the Christ; (b) all must have been witnesses of His resurrection; and (c) all were to have been chosen by Him to launch the gospel and to have a part in the foundation of the Church:

> "And are built upon the foundation of the apostles and prophets, Jesus Christ himself being the chief corner stone" (Ephesians 2:20).

Judas Iscaraiot was replaced, according to prophecy, while the eleven waited in the Upper Room:

> "Wherefore of these men which have companied with us all the time that the Lord Jesus went in and out among us,
>
> "Beginning from the baptism of John, unto that same day that he was taken up from us, must one be ordained to be witness with us of his resurrection . . . .
>
> "And they gave forth their lots; and the lot fell upon Matthias; and he was numbered with the eleven apostles" (Acts 1:21, 22, 26).

As for Paul's apostleship, the Scriptures bear record of his call on the road to Damascus and that which followed. Lying in the dust, blinded by God's glory—"he trembling and astonished said, Lord, what wilt thou have me to do? And the Lord said unto him, Arise, and go into the city, and it shall be told thee what thou must do" (Acts 9:6). In the city, God had moved on Ananias, who was the one to tell him what he must do. Of this Church-persecuting Saul of Tarsus, God said:

> " . . . He is a chosen vessel unto me, to bear my name before the Gentiles, and kings, and the children of Israel" (Acts 9:15).

It all came to pass; and it became necessary for him to defend his apostleship.

> "And last of all he [Jesus] was seen of me also, as of one born out of due time.
>
> "For I am the least of the apostles, that am not meet to be called an apostle, because I persecuted the church of God.
>
> "But by the grace of God I am what I am . . . " (1 Corinthians 15:8-19).

> "Am I not an apostle? . . . have I not seen . . . the Lord?
>
> "If I am not an apostle unto others, yet doubtless I am to you: for the seal of mine apostleship are ye in the Lord" (1 Corinthians 9:1, 2; also see Romans 1:1, 2 and 1 Corinthians 1:1).

Certainly **as Saul** he was not seeking the office; nor did he seek it **as Paul.** He counted himself "less than the least of all saints" (Ephesians 3:8).

Humility, not self-exaltation, is the mark of any true minister. Those professing "apostles" at Ephesus could not qualify. Paul had warned the elders of this church that false professors would arise in their midst (Acts 20:29-31); and the church had heeded the warning, as Jesus Himself testified of them in this letter some thirty-six years later. Apparently, in the context of the words, "and hast borne, and hast patience," there is reference to the fair trial the church had given these imposters. "Tried," as used in verse two, indicates a fair investigation of their claims, and the discovery that those claims were false. The church had not acted impulsively and rashly with them. (See the notes on "patience" under (2) above in this lesson.)

(5) **He knew it was for His name's sake they had labored—**". . . and for my name's sake hast laboured, and hast not fainted." The statement probably includes the labors in patience and long endurance through the years, not merely in this or that isolated instance. (See notes on "labors" under (1) above in this lesson.) Though the pastor and saints at Ephesus could not tolerate men known to be evil, still they could labor in the right causes without fainting; perhaps to save those who had been influenced and deceived by those evil men and false apostles.

It is a pleasure to labor "for Jesus' sake" once we have actually seen Him at Calvary and have the proper heart-response to His finished work ON OUR BEHALF. In this light, we can more clearly see what a single soul, or a right cause, means to Him who died for that soul or that cause.

The One Indictment

"Nevertheless I have *somewhat* against thee, because thou hast left thy first love" (Revelation 2:4).

The word "somewhat" in this verse is in italics, indicating that it was inserted by the translator. Expositors of the original text say that this "unwarrantably softens the censure." It was a "grave thing," not an insignificant "somewhat." They had allowed that holy love and zeal for Christ to decline in an alarming measure.

Does the Love they had left mean "thy love for the brethren"?

More probably, "thy love for me" (Christ). The bride-bridegroom relationship was a familiar one from Paul's explanation in Ephesians 5:23-33. It is probably this love on the part of the espoused bride that is intended here. He who walks among the candlesticks with the stars in His hand sees, and impartially evaluates, both the good and the bad; the virtues and the blemishes.

The word "left" (not "lost") means abandoned: "To leave, or desert; to give up completely." The accusation is a sad commentary on this church to whom Paul had written thirty-two years before, "Wherefore I also, after I heard of your faith in the Lord Jesus, and love unto all the saints, cease not to give thanks for you, making mention of you in my prayers" (Ephesians 1:15, 16).

These now were "second generation Christians." In this sense, as a whole congregation they may have done what has been common through the years among churches everywhere. Following a period of great revival or renewal through an outpouring of the Holy Ghost by way of vivid gospel preaching, there was a flood of love for Christ and everyone else. There was a holy zeal to labor for Him in every area of Christian service, from outreach and soul-winning to the establishing of the local church as a lighthouse among dying men and women. But little by little the zeal cooled and apathy replaced it. The importance of "the weightier matters . . . judgment, mercy, and faith . . . .and the love of God" (Matthew 23:23 and Luke 11:42) diminished. Like those Pharisees Jesus addressed, they kept up their good works—almsgiving, tithe-paying, fasting twice a week, abstinence from extortion, unjust dealings and adultery (Luke 18:11, 12), and much more—but almost altogether in a mechanical attitude of traditional loyalty and faithfulness, not from a heart of burning love. This church had **labored** patiently "for Jesus' sake," but they were no longer **loving** for Jesus' sake!

Again we ask: **Is it possible to labor for Christ's sake without a love He can accept?** Here was a congregation duly commended for its **labors,** yet warned of pending removal for **a defective love.** A little sober thought will remind us that we can be in love with our own "system"—our planned procedures and cherished goals—more than with the Christ whose name continues to cling to our tongues! doing, doing, doing; feverishly laboring; proud of "exceeding last year's accomplishments"—100% in reaching our own marks! All of this, only to be reproved for having a misplaced love!

Some Possible Causes

Among the suggested causes for this church having left their first love are the following five:

(1) **The boredom of routine**—a problem which churches in every age have had to guard against. This routine may include, among other things, a "bookplanned" program devoid of fresh inspiration; a "rut" of repetition. Sometimes it may even be "fiery" repetition—a sort of "learned" procedure; an effort to MAKE a service vibrant rather than LET it be vibrant by the power of the Holy Ghost. " Borrowed," warmed-over sermons (discourses) which have no relevance to the current need, can be boring to a congregation whose real needs are not being met.

"Standing somewhere in the shadows you'll find Jesus," as the well-intentioned chorus says, can be sadly all too true. Would He not prefer to freely "walk in our midst"? The Holy Ghost should never be put "on hold," and made to wait for an opportunity to bless in His own way.

The real blessing God has in store might be in the preaching of the Word. Sometimes His "still small voice" is a boredom-shattering break from the "strong wind . . . earthquake . . . fire" routine (1 Kings 19:11, 12). Water (the Spirit) is vital, but a hungry congregation must have bread and meat (the Word).

(2) **The "curse" of prosperity**—which can so easily turn our trust and thanksgiving in the wrong direction. "The love of money . . . the root of all evil" (1 Timothy 6:10) replaces our love for the giver. This usually leads on to a love for the world and its "things": (1 John 2:15)—a satisfaction with the temporal rather than the eternal (2 Corinthians 4:18); a seeking for food, drink, and raiment, or laying plans for "tomorrow," when Jesus has said, "But seek ye first the kingdom of God, and his righteousness; and all these things shall be added unto you" (Matthew 6:33). So many "things" —even our loved ones—can be turned into "idols," in the sense of being loved and served ahead of God!

(3) **An education obsession**—which the enemy looks upon as a vantage point to direct our dependence away from the guidance and unction of the Holy Ghost. This need not be so,

of course, but without doubt, it has drawn many souls away from their "first love." A good, basic education is not to be demeaned, but at the same time, the dangers must not be left untold. So-called Bible courses that are more "men's inventions" (Ecclesiastes 7:29; Psalms 106:29, 39) than Bible may be even more destructive than secular courses in "science falsely so called" (1 Timothy 6:20). When education puts orthodoxy ahead of "the knowledge of his will in all wisdom and spiritual understanding" (Colossians 1:9), the Holy Ghost is deprived of His work of revealing "the deep things of God" (1 Corinthians 2:10; read verses 9 through 16).

(4) **Love turned inward**—a gradual shifting of the emphasis onto loving the Church, and God's and Christ's love for us, with only a token expression of our love for God and His Son. We know we should love Him. We may feel guilty because we know in our hearts that we should bear greater substantial evidence of that love. We may try to compensate by offering frequent praise; lip-service as a part of the "routine" described above.

We would be shocked to discover that these "traditional" gestures border closely on that which Jesus saw as hypocrisy in the scribes and Pharisees: "Well hath Esaias prophesied of you hypocrites, as it is written, This people honoureth me with their lips, but their heart is far from me. Howbeit in vain do they worship me . . . " (Mark 7:6, 7).

Christ's love was always outgoing. He so loved the Church that He gave Himself for it (Ephesians 5:25). The question is always one to be reckoned with: **Does the Church love the Bridegroom more than herself?**

(5) **Doctrinal dogmatism at the expense of joyful obedience**—the motivation of legalism rather than of love. A harsh spirit of "law" can smother out the blessed free spirit of grace. A rigid imposition of "the letter" demands in turn the imposition of penalties and punishments. Soon an unbending discipline is seen as more important than "speaking the truth in love" (Ephesians 4:15) in order that the weak and unlearned may be wooed, nourished, and strengthened. The doctrine is important, and it is to be respected, but problems arise when there is a misplaced emphasis.

(6) Last, but by no means least, **too little communion with the Lord.** As a rule, we arrange to spend much time with those we love. Christ desires our communion in prayer and

the study of the Word. When our times of communion with Him grow shorter and less frequent, it is evident that our love has grown cold. Other things tend to demand our prayer periods. Other reading matter begins to interest us more than the Bible. We would rather socialize—feed the body on knick-knacks and the mind and soul on "harmless pleasures" (Profitless, too!) than to fast on "the riches of his grace." Fellowship with the saints is scriptural, but communion with God is absolutely necessary for the maintenance of spiritual life and growth.

The church at Ephesus undoubtedly had some measure of love; perhaps even more than the average congregation today; but if so, it was an inferior, unsatisfactory love in God's sight. The indictment was more than a casual "tap on the wrist"; more than a mild reproof; more than a passing criticism as though they were making "a passing grade" when they were capable of an A-plus—as we shall see.

ADMONITION, EXHORTATION, AND CONSEQUENCES

"Remember therefore from whence thou art fallen, and repent, and do the first works . . . " (Revelation 2:5).

A Three-fold Charge

(1) **Remember.** Since the indictment was a diminishing love, Christ charged them to remember that first love from which they had departed, or the heights of love from which they had descended. **Adam Clarke** has put it well:

Consider the state of grace in which you once stood; the happiness, love, and joy which you felt when you received remission of sins; the zeal you had for God's glory and the salvation of mankind; your willing, obedient spirit, your cheerful self-denial, your fervor in private prayer, your detachment from the world, and your heavenly-mindedness. Remember—consider, all these.

Matthew Henry enhances Clarke's considerations:

"They must consider how much better it was with them then than now; how much peace, strength, purity, and pleasure they had lost by leaving their first love;—how much more comfortably they could lie down and sleep at night—how much more cheerfully they could awake in the morning—how much better they could bear afflictions, and how much more becomingly they could enjoy the favors of Providence—how much easier the thoughts of death were to them, and how much stronger their desires and hopes of heaven.

In so remembering, they possibly would consider that those first emotional, zealous feelings should have deepened to permanence rather than waning.

(2) **Repent.** If their remembering was sincere, and if it stirred a desire to experience those things again, the reasonable response would be repentance. And if the repentance was sincere, it would spring from a sense of conviction and remorse upon realizing that it was the loving Christ of Calvary that they had neglected and come to take for granted.

They would be inwardly grieved and ashamed at the thought of their having come to the place where they simply did that which was their duty to do (Luke 17:10)—perhaps even claiming merit which belonged strictly to Christ. An unbiased self-examination would surely lead to a right-about-face repentance.

(3) **Do the first works.** Repentance is only a word unless it effects a change of behavior. The Ephesians' "first works" as a follow up of true repentance meant those things which had accompanied their "first love"—confession, restitution, water baptism; works that were inspired and motivated by a fervent love for Him who had satisfied their sin-debt by suffering their death penalty. Paul has said it so well in a few words:

> "For though he was crucified through weakness [as a man for men], yet he liveth [having conquered death] by the power of God. For we also are weak in him, but we shall live with him by the power of God toward you" (2 Corinthians 13:4).

O what motivation to render loving service to Him until their dying breath! Yet they had "left" that first love. But a rekindling of the fire of love would bring back the fire of those first works.

Needless to say, no man's good works can save him. The

works that save are Christ's works. The believer does good works because he is saved, and the love of Christ constrains him to render the service of sincere appreciation with pure delight.

The Consequences

"... Or else [if you do not remember, repent, and do the first works] I will come unto thee quickly, and will remove thy candlestick out of his place, except thou repent" (Revelation 2:5).

The Lord does not make empty threats. This was a positive pronouncement of sudden, surprising judgment that would surely come unless they heeded Christ's personal warning. Since we learned in the beginning that the candlestick was the church, it is clear that the removal of this local church is meant. Some have queried whether the church would have been destroyed or simply moved to another place. But if their love was defective, moving them twenty or a hundred miles down the road would hardly have corrected the problem. It seems more probable that the cessation of the church's existence is to be understood.

We can only speculate as to how this might come about; but Jesus said it would be done "quickly" once He began the removal. Circumstances can quickly arise and develop, in the absence of love, which could bring about what we refer to as the disbandment of a local church. Christ's judgments are just. A church that is not a living, loving testimony for Him in a community is a reproach to Him in that community. It would be better that it not be there.

ONE FINAL COMMENDATION

"But this thou hast [in thy favor], that thou hatest the deeds of the Nicolaitanes, which I also hate" (Revelation 2:6).

He did not hate the individuals **as souls** who held this heresy, but **their deeds.** The Nicolaitanes have been variously described, both their origin and their error. As to their origin, two possibilities have been offered: (1) That their name was derived from two Greek words—**nikao,** meaning "to conquer," and **laos,** meaning "the people"; therefore, "the conquering of the people." It was held by some that this sect was the forerunner of the imposition of the clerical hierarchy which later robbed the laity of their spiritual freedom. (2) That the founder was "Nicolas a proselyte of Antioch," one of the seven men selected as deacons (Acts 6:3-6), but who had turned heretic. This is the prevailing opinion among many credible expositors.

As to their error, the Nicolaitanes' hateful deeds were highly licentious. **Irenaeus,** one of the Early Church fathers, says: "The Nicolaitanes . . . lead lives of unrestrained indulgences . . . ." **Adam Clarke** is more analytical:

> There were, it is commonly supposed, a sect of Gnostics, who taught the most impure doctrines, and followed the most impure practices . . . [they] taught the community [plurality] of wives, that adultery and fornication were things indifferent, that eating meats offered to idols was quite lawful; and mixed several pagan rites with the Christian ceremonies . . . .

(NOTE: The Gnostics made up a pagan heresy known as Gnosticism, of which the Nicolaitanes were one branch, or school. The word **gnosis** means knowledge. This sect took a morbid pride in knowledge, placing an over-evaluation on it, with a depreciation of faith [Romans 1:22]. They considered themselves "the intellectual aristocracy," or "a higher class" in the Church [**Schaff's History of the Christian Church.** Vol. II, pages 445, 446]. They were dualistic in that certain elements represented two opposite extremes: [a] **aceticism,** an austere, prideful, self-denying lifestyle, based on the abhorrence of the body of flesh [Colossians 2:23]; and [b] **antinomianism,** a "believe God and do as you please" philosophy. The Nicolaitanes were of this second school of thought.)

THE PROMISE TO THE OVERCOMER

Following His admonition, "He that hath an ear, let him hear what the Spirit saith unto the churches," (see remarks on this passage in Lesson Two), Christ extended a precious promise:

> " . . . To him [singular and personal] that overcometh will I give to eat of the tree of life, which is in the midst

of the paradise of God" (Revelation 2:7).

The Ephesian saints had much in their favor; yet the one indictment was of such weight that it could deprive them of heaven. This promise reminded them that it was possible to overcome that failure; possible to remain true and stedfast in the face of "them which are evil"—the false apostles, and the licentious Nicolaitanes. If there were any of these among the membership, they were contributing to the waning love, and to the possibility of the removal of that local church from the presence of Him who walked among the churches. Perhaps they recalled Jesus' words to the apostles, since John (who had sent this letter) was one of them, and had been an ear-witness—

"And many false prophets shall rise, and shall deceive many.
"And because iniquity shall abound, the love of many shall wax cold.
"But he that shall endure unto the end [overcome; conquer], the same shall be saved" (Matthew 24:11-13).

Perhaps they had also read Paul's words of encouragement to the Romans—yea, he may have spoken these words to them when he was with them:

"Who shall separate us from the love of Christ? shall tribulation, or distress, or persecution, or famine, or nakedness, or peril, or sword?
"Nay, in all these things [suffering; trials] we are more than conquerors through him that loved us.
"For I am persuaded, that neither death, nor life, nor angels, nor principalities, nor powers, nor things present, nor things to come,
"Nor height, nor depth, nor any other creature, shall be able to separate us from the love of God, which is in Christ Jesus our Lord" (Romans 8:35, 37-39).

While unity is precious, needful, and helpful, if it is broken by contention or sin in the local church, the individual who overcomes will not be forsaken or cast off. By the grace of God we are "more than conquerors," more than "overcomers";

not by our own strength, nor by our own holiness, but "through him that loved us"!

Death was inherited from Adam, and he was expelled from the garden and the tree of life (Genesis 3:22-24). But life is restored by Him who IS the LIFE! Hallelujah! In Him we have eaten of the tree of life; and out there beyond this "vail of tears," and beyond the Millennium, in the blessed "new earth," we will rejoice to see "in the midst of the street of it, and on either side of the river . . . the tree of life . . . " (Revelation 22:2)!

"Paradise" has always meant the place of rest for those who depart this temporal life at peace with God. Abraham was there (Luke 16:22), and he is still there awaiting reunion with his body at the resurrection of the just (Luke 14:14; Revelation 20:4-6). Job is awaiting the change to incorruption and immortality (Job 14:13-15; 1 Corinthians 15:51-58). And the promise is to every one who endures to the end!

Overcomers at last—and forever!

LISTENING TO THE LETTER

The Ephesians Listened

Imagine the saints at Ephesus as they had gathered to hear their pastor read to them a letter from Christ, sent to them by their beloved Apostle John. None of them except John had seen the Christ, except by faith; but how must this pastor have felt to be told that he was being held in Christ's right hand! And how must that congregation have felt to be reminded that He was walking in their midst! Surely they must have sensed His presence that day!

Even if there was an evil element among them, who had lied about a false apostleship, or who had lived by the abominable teachings of the Nicolaitanes, they must have felt that Presence, but in fear and conviction and pending judgment!

As for the church as a whole, even before the one indictment was pronounced they may have begun to feel the shame of the "mechanical" works, "carried out" faithfully, but dutifully, with little thought of their original motivation. Then—yes, they heard it—"Thou hast left thy first love"!

Perhaps tears were flowing now. Possibly the "repentance" had already begun. Surely from this day forth there would be "revival"—a return to the "first love" they had left behind—maybe years before!

The Ephesian saints apparently profited from this letter, for history shows that that church continued functioning for many years. Of course, after the Nicean Council in A.D. 325, the true Church of God went into the Dark Ages, and the status of those who remained faithful in their hearts we must leave with the all-knowing God. The city of Ephesus gradually declined after the fifth century A.D., until finally, in the fourteenth century, the remaining inhabitants were deported elsewhere.

(NOTE: Incidentally, history says that John returned to Ephesus after his exile ended, and that he died there during the time of the Roman Emperor Trajan—perhaps in the year A.D. 98. Though Symeon, bishop of Jerusalem and James' successor, was crucified, and Ignatius, bishop of Antioch, was thrown to the wild beasts in the Roman Colosseum during Trajan's rule (**Schaff's History of the Christian Church**), God saw fit that John should die a natural death.

Are WE Listening?

Now, imagine our own local church receiving this same personal letter from Christ Jesus our Lord, dictated to, and written by, the hand of some dear brother in the Lord in whom we have the utmost confidence. What might be our response?

Do pastors today sincerely believe they are in His loving but almighty hand? Do they understand that, while they have His care and protection and providence, He can (though sadly and regretfully) cast them aside? (Read 1 Corinthians 9:19-27.)

Are the members of the Church made aware, by this letter, that loveless service profits nothing, but rather invites destruction? God is not "out to destroy us" the moment we err in the least. He is "out to save us" from ourselves, and from the deceptions of the grievous wolves that "enter in," or from those men from our own ranks who "arise . . . to draw away disciples after them" (Acts 20:29, 30). He loves those "wolves" and "inside deceivers" enough to warn them of their end; and He loves the innocent or gullible ones of us too much to let us continue our "production line" type of service, scarcely having Him in mind at all.

Even our worship can become mere habit—that "happy rut" we have traveled in so long that we simply stay in it thoughtlessly. It is possible to sing and re-sing words and melodies without true heart-praise. But is that the way we worshipped when we had just experienced our "first love"? As Paul often said, "GOD FORBID!" We can never praise Him enough, of course. But—"a barrel of saccharin is worth less than one drop of pure honey."

Likewise, we can "work our fingers to the bone" for the Church, all the while giving lip-service to "Jesus' name," yet He may know that we would do much less, or nothing, were it not for the recognition of men. More often we "love the Church" because the Church is "US." But our "first love" was not "self-love." It was "self-sacrificing" love. It was LOVE FOR HIM!

Will your pastor and mine, your local church and mine, retain that "first love," with the candlestick still in place when Jesus returns to present the Church unto Himself? If not, will you and I, as individual members, be found overcomers? As the old Hymn, "Hold the Fort," concludes—

"BY THY GRACE WE WILL!"

—Lesson Four—

THE CHURCH AT SMYRNA

RELATION OF CITY AND CHURCH

The Geographical, Cultural, and Historical Situation

Geography: Smyrna was located about thirty-five miles north of Ephesus, off the Aegean Sea on the Bay of Smyrna, which gave it a well-protected harbor and a terminal for a trade route up the Hermus River. It was in the district of Lydia, beautifully situated at the foot of a low mountain named Pagos, which at one time was the acropolis of the city. The modern name for Smyrna is Izmir, and it is Turkey's largest port.

Culture and History: According to the **Thompson Bible Survey,** Smyrna was founded by the Greeks as an Ionian colony about 1000 B.C. Its history includes periods of destruction by other powers. In 600 B.C. it was destroyed by a Lydian devastation, and was not rebuilt for three centuries. It came under Roman rule in 27 B.C.

Like Ephesus, it had a "religious" history. One commentator in **The Pulpit Commentary** says: "When eleven cities of Asia competed for the honor of erecting a temple to Tiberius [Caesar], the senate decided in favor of Smyrna. This temple was no doubt standing in St. John's time. But just as Artemis [Diana] was the great goddess of the Ephesians, so Dionysus was the great god of Smyrna. Dionysus represented the mysteriously productive and intoxicating powers of nature . . . hence the myth of his death and resurrection . . . ." History also records Dionysus as the Greek god of vegetation and wine, and is identified with the Roman god Bacchus.

Some suppose that Apostle Paul first introduced Christianity in Smyrna during the time of his three-year ministry at Ephesus. However, since there is no record of such in Acts, it could have been evangelized by someone who fled Jerusalem when the Church fell under persecution there. (Read Acts 8:1-4.) The first biblical mention of a church at Smyrna is that made by John. It is thought that Polycarp, John's pupil and contemporary minister, was the "angel" of the church to whom John sent the letter. (See further details under "Listening to the Letter," this lesson.)

John F. Walvoord says that Smyrna today is still a large city and has a Christian church. It is said that one-third of the two hundred thousand population are Christians.

CHRIST INTRODUCES HIMSELF

"And unto the angel of the church in Smyrna write; These things saith the first and the last, which was dead, and is alive" (Revelation 2:8).

All that Christ is, through His oneness with the Father in the total revelation (Revelation 1:17, 18), He is to the local body of saints. He is the King Eternal—"Now unto the King eternal, immortal, invisible, the only wise God, be honour and glory for ever and ever. Amen" (1 Timothy 1:17).

He is "The first and the last" in that "he is before **all things,** and by him **all things** consist" (Colossians 1:17); "Jesus Christ the same yesterday, and today, and for ever" (Hebrews 13:8).

This also encompasses the statements that He "was dead; and is alive." The fact that He at one time "was dead" presupposes that prior to His death He was alive. Peter, writing of our redemption, declares that the price was—

"... With the precious blood of Christ, as of a lamb without blemish and without spot:
"Who verily was foreordained before the foundation of the world ... " (1 Peter 1:19, 20).

"... The works were finished from the foundation of the world" (Hebrews 4:3).

In John's Gospel we read of Jesus talking with the Father about their relationship before He came into the world at Bethlehem:

"And now, O Father, glorify thou me with thine own self with the glory which I had with thee before the world was.
"For thou lovedst me before the foundation of the world" (John 17:5, 24).

He was the bodily manifestation of God, the great "I AM" of Exodus 3:14. Time after time He confirmed this while He dwelt among men:

"... Verily, verily, I say unto you, Before Abraham was, I am" (John 8:58).

"I am the bread of life...." (John 6:35); "I am the light of the world" (John 8:12); "I am the way, the truth, and the life" (John 14:6); "I am the door of the sheep... the good shepherd" (John 10:7, 9, 11); "because I said, I am the Son of God" (John 10:36); "I am the resurrection, and the life" (John 11:25); "Ye call me Master and Lord... so I am" (John 13:13); "I am the true vine" (John 15:1).

Then consider the Holy Ghost-inspired record concerning the WORD in the beginning:

"In the beginning was the Word, and the Word was with God, and the Word was God.
"The same was in the beginning with God.
"All things were made by him; and without him was not any thing made that was made.
"And the Word was made flesh, and dwelt among us..." (John 1:1-3, 14).

As the Son of man, with the sins of the whole world upon Him, and suffering OUR condemnation, "... he was crucified through weakness, yet he liveth by the power of God" (2 Corinthians 13:4). He submitted Himself unto death in order that He might be victorious over death FOR US (1 Corinthians 15:54-57; 2 Corinthians 4:10, 11; 1 Peter 3:18, 19; Philippians 2:8; 2 Timothy 1:10; Hebrews 2:9, 10; 1 Corinthians 15:1-23).

He who from everlasting was LIFE took on a body of flesh that could die, "that through death he might destroy him that had the power of death, that is, the devil" (Hebrews 2:14). He laid down His life willingly and deliberately. No man took it from Him against His will. Read it in His own words:

"Therefore doth my Father love me, because I lay down my life, that I might take it [up] again.
"No man taketh it from me, but I lay it down of myself. I have power [the right and authority] to lay it

down, and I have power [the right and authority] to take it [up] again. This commandment [appointment] have I received of my Father" (John 10:17, 18).

This particular introduction of Himself as the Eternal Victor was probably for the purpose of giving courage to this church which was being, and would be, tested and tried by tribulation, poverty, imprisonment, and the blasphemy of professed Jews (verses 9, 10). Even the name "Smyrna" meant "myrrh," which symbolized Christ's suffering and death in His humanity. He thus reminded them that He had suffered and died for the Church because He loved it. He could be touched with the feeling of their every infirmity because He was "in all points tempted as we are, yet without sin" (Hebrews 4:15). Now, if they would willingly suffer with Him, they would also reign with Him (2 Timothy 2:12).

CHRIST'S APPROVAL OF THE CHURCH

"I know thy works, and tribulation, and poverty, (but thou art rich) . . . " (Revelation 2:9).

The problems this church had were external, since there is no word of dissatisfaction pronounced against it. Christ's commendations included:

(1) **Endurance in tribulations:** speculations vary as to the source and nature of their "tribulations":

(a) In this city steeped in idolatry and emporer worship, there was undoubtedly great aversion to Christianity and its pure standard of life. Believers were probably considered disruptive and divisive. In a move for political favor from Rome, a temple had been built in A.D. 26 in honor of the "deity" of the Emperor Tiberius. Little by little, emperor worship had proceeded from "voluntary" to "mandatory." Since every citizen, at least once a year, was required to say, "Caesar is lord," Christians were branded "enemies of the state" because they refused to acknowledge any "Lord" except Christ. Other religions allowed this token worship of the emperor, because they could do so and then continue their worship of any god they desired. Of course, the members of the church would not submit to this double-minded compromise.

(b) The Christians' withdrawal from the prevalently secular, immoral society and its lifestyles may have brought persecutions from those who thought these believers felt themselves better than others. The nature of such persecutions may have ranged from the loss of friends to outright acts of violence.

(c) Then, there were the provocative Jews, which we will consider presently.

(2) **Endurance in poverty:** Poverty, in the context here, derives from a word which denotes **an abject poverty**—a miserable, wretched lack of temporal goods. One commentator has observed that to be "poor among the poor" would have been a trial in itself, but to be "poor among the rich" was a greater test. It no doubt entailed being slighted and demeaned as a "lower class"; perhaps as a burden on a society which was reluctant to show charity.

Then there was the actual want, or need; the struggle to meet the bare necessities of everyday life. It has been suggested that this resulted as a part of their persecution, possibly in the form of excess taxation, or in being overpowered and robbed by ransacking factions. If so, their poverty contributed to their tribulations, and vice versa.

Some of these saints may at one time have been wealthy, but upon conversion had found that they could not continue in some offensive occupation which had provided sufficient income; so they had forsaken it all to be Christ's disciples (Luke 14:33). Like Moses, they esteemed "the reproach of Christ greater riches than the treasures of Egypt [the world]" (Hebrews 11:26). And unlike the rich, young ruler, they were ready and willing to "sell all they had," as it were, rather than be rejected by Christ (Matthew 19:16-30).

But Jesus, after saying He knew their poverty, was quick to add, "but thou art rich." No one could say this with as great authority as He, of whom it is written, "For ye know the grace of our Lord Jesus Christ, that, though he was rich, yet for your sakes he became poor, that ye through his poverty might be rich" (2 Corinthians 8:9). This same High Authority had said, in His "Sermon on the Mount":

> "Lay not up for yourselves treasures upon earth, where moth and rust doth corrupt, and where thieves break through and steal:
>
> "But lay up for yourselves treasures in heaven, where neither moth nor rust doth corrupt, and where thieves

do not break through nor steal:
"For where your treasure is, there will your heart be also" (Matthew 6:19-21).

Later, He warned of the deceitfulness of riches (Matthew 13:22). According to Solomon, this deceitfulness crops out through "fair-weather friends": "Wealth maketh many friends, but the poor is separated from his neighbor" (Proverbs 19:4; see also Proverbs 14:20).

Perhaps the pastor at Smyrna had heard of Paul's words of encouragement to the ministry—

"But in all things approving ourselves as the ministers of God, in much patience, in afflictions, in necessities, in distresses,

"... As poor, yet making many rich; as having nothing, and yet possessing all things" (2 Corinthians 6:4, 10).

Perhaps also they had read James' words concerning God's love for the poor:

"Hearken, my beloved brethren, Hath not God chosen the poor of this world rich in faith, and heirs of the kingdom which he hath promised to them that love him?" (James 2:5).

In his fifth chapter, James rebukes the rich, and once again consoles the poor who are oppressed by them:

"Go to now, ye rich men, weep and howl for your miseries that shall come upon you.

"Your riches are corrupted, and your garments are motheaten.

"Your gold and silver is cankered; and the rust of them shall be a witness against you, and shall eat your flesh as it were fire. Ye have heaped treasure together for the last days (your old age).

"Behold, the hire of the labourers who have reaped down your fields, which is of you kept back by fraud, crieth: and the cries of them which have reaped are entered into the ears of the Lord of sabaoth.

"Ye have lived in pleasure on the earth, and been

wanton; ye have nourished your hearts, as in a day of slaughter.

"Ye have condemned and killed the just; and he doth not resist you.

"Be patient therefore, brethren, unto the coming of the Lord.

Behold, the husbandman waiteth for the precious fruit of the earth, and hath long patience for it, until he receive the early and latter rain.

"Be ye also patient; stablish your hearts: for the coming of the Lord draweth nigh" (James 5:1-8).

David has said: "A little that a righteous man hath is better than the riches of many wicked" (Psalms 37:16); also, "The fear of the Lord is clean, enduring for ever: the judgments of the Lord are true and righteous altogether. More to be desired are they than gold, yea, than much fine gold . . ." (Psalms 19:9, 10). (See also Proverbs 11:4; 15:16; 16:16; 17:1; 19:1; 28:6.)

The Apostle Paul comforts the poor and charges the rich in the following words, which are so very relevant today:

"Perverse disputings of men of corrupt minds, and destitute of the truth, supposing that gain is godliness ["God wants you rich and prosperous," say the positive thinkers]: from such withdraw thyself.

"But godliness with contentment is great gain.

"For we brought nothing into this world, and it is certain we can carry nothing out.

"And having food and raiment let us be therewith content.

"But they that will be rich fall into temptation and a snare, and into many foolish and hurtful lusts, which drown men in destruction and perdition.

"For the love of money is the root of all evil: which while some coveted after, they have erred from the faith, and pierced themselves through with many sorrows.

"But thou, O man of God, flee these things; and follow after righteousness, godliness, faith, love, patience, meekness . . . .

"Charge them that are rich in this world, that they be not highminded, nor trust in uncertain riches, but in

the living God, who giveth us richly all things to enjoy;
"That they do good, that they be rich in good works, ready to distribute, willing to communicate;"
"Laying up in store for themselves a good foundation against the time to come, that they may lay hold on eternal life" (1 Timothy 6:5-11, 17-19).

Wealth is permissible, but it can be dangerous if it becomes our trust. In all their poverty, regardless of the cause, Jesus saw the saints at Smyrna as rich, because their works were unreproveable in His sight.

The blasphemous Jews

"... And I know the blasphemy of them which say they are Jews, and are not, but are of the synagogue of Satan" (Revelation 2:9).

Webster defines blasphemy as: "Profane or mocking speech, writing, or action concerning God or anything regarded as sacred; contempt [scorn; disrespect] for God ... deliberately mocking or contemptuous of God." **Cruden's Concordance** adds that it means intentional indignity.

First, let us identify these blasphemers. Opinions vary. They may have been the Jewish element that opposed Christianity and the Church everywhere the gospel message was preached. The apostles and others, such as Stephen and Philip, met this opposition in every city.

The Jews as a whole had rejected Christ, and in turn all who preached Him. They continued their synagogue form of worship, even though God had fulfilled in Christ everything pertaining to the old order. It was a dead system so far as God was concerned, and the apostles had turned away from the resistant Jews to the receptive Gentiles. By their very action of continuing the form of that which Christ had fulfilled, they were blaspheming God. They were acting in contempt of God's Word and will, all of which had been declared in the law and the prophets. In striking out against Christ and His Church, they were striking out at God. Jesus had said, "He that is not with me is against me; and he that gathereth not with me scattereth abroad" (Matthew 12:30). Those who take a stand against Christ are for Satan. Therefore, those blaspheming Jews, in Jesus' words, were "the synagogue of Satan."

The true Jew recognized the new dispensation of Christ as the continuing outworking of the overall plan of God. And there were some true Jews who believed and continued in the advancing light. Israel, as a whole, violated their status as God's chosen people when they refused to continue in His revealed order—the Church. They went on claiming to be Jews, though they had denied their identity in fulfilled prophecy.

Jesus said they "say they are Jews, and are not." Thus it is clear that regardless of who they were, or what they said, He knew they were not truly Jews. Their false claim amounted to blasphemy.

Paul made some statements which may apply to the situation at Smyrna. In Romans, chapter 2, he declares that "there is no respect of persons with God" (verse 11), going on to show that the true "circumcision"—the chosen and sealed people of God—are those who are **doers,** and not **hearers** only (verses 13-15 and 25-29). In verse 17 he says, "Behold, thou art called a Jew." Then he puts questions to them which, if answered truthfully, would bring them to a very sobering conclusion:

". . . He is not a Jew, which is one outwardly; neither is that circumcision, which is outward in the flesh:

"But he is a Jew, which is one inwardly; and circumcision is that of the heart, in the spirit, and not in the letter; whose praise is not of men, but of God" (Romans 2:28, 29).

In verse 24 he accuses those professing Jews of blaspheming the name of God in the eyes of the Gentiles by failing to be what they claimed to be. He apparently was addressing the same problem when he wrote to the Philippians:

"Beware of dogs, beware of evil workers, beware of the concision.

"For we are the circumcision [Jew and Gentile] which worship God in the spirit, and rejoice in Christ Jesus, and have no confidence in the flesh" (Philippians 3:2, 3).

"Dogs" was a term of reproach. Ordinarily it was used by the Jews to refer to all Gentiles, but here Paul uses it in referring to those Jews who reproached Christ and the gospel through their rejection of Him, and by their constant opposition to the gospel. He warns the Philippian saints to beware of these "evil workers"—the "concision."

The "concision" has its roots in a pagan corruption of circumcision of the flesh, which was a mutilation that pagan worshippers inflicted upon themselves. (See 1 Kings 18:28 for a similarity.) **Kenneth S. Wuest** says, "The Judaizers mutilated the message of the Gospel by adding law to grace, and thus [mutilated] their own spiritual lives and those of their converts." Paul uses the word to distinguish the spiritual circumcision of the heart from the mere ceremonial form, which is now extinct.

God originated circumcision with Abraham before the law, as a seal of the Abrahamic Covenant, which was a covenant of promise—or of faith in God's promise. Writing to the churches of Galatia about the problem of the Judaizers, Paul elaborates somewhat on the blessing of Abraham being for the Gentiles as well as for the Jews. He says that this was the gospel, which was preached to Abraham by way of that covenant (Galatians 3:8, 9). In a nutshell, he says, "For ye are all [both Jews and Gentiles] the children of God by faith in Christ Jesus . . . .And if ye be Christ's, then are ye Abraham's seed, and heirs according to the promise" (Galatians 3:26, 29; read the entire chapter).

To the Galatians he also explains that the "new creature" —the heart-changed, justified believer—takes the place of the circumcision (the chosen according to the flesh), and the heart-circumcized body of believers in Christ are now "the Israel of God' (Galatians 6:15, 16), making up the Church.

Another speculation is that the blaspheming Jews were professed Christians whom Jesus knew were not. If so, they must have been something like a denominational group, or even a cult, which functioned outside the church; otherwise, Christ would have had to reprove the church at Smyrna for allowing them to remain in the body.

ADMONITION AND EXHORTATION

"Fear none of those things which thou shalt suffer:

behold, the devil shall cast some of you into prison, that ye may be tried; and ye shall have tribulation ten days . . . " (Revelation 2:10).

Exhortation Against Fear of Suffering

The original wording is: "Stop being afraid of the things you are about to be suffering." This shows that the saints at least had forebodings of things that would be unpleasant and hard to bear, even beyond the "tribulation, and poverty" they were already experiencing. Jesus proceeded to give some specifics:

(1) "The devil shall cast some of you into prison, that ye may be tried." No doubt that "synagogue of Satan" would be instrumental in this; but the devil uses any available channel to attack God and His Church. He will use any excuse at all to bring accusation against God's people.

But, while the devil cast these saints into prison in a show of power and domination over them, Jesus said that the purpose was "that ye may be tried." God allowed their imprisonment, knowing it could turn to them for a testimony of faith and overcoming grace. This same Jesus, while on His earthly sojourn, spoke the following words to His disciples when they had inquired of the signs of the latter days:

" . . . They shall lay their hands on you, and persecute you, delivering you up to the synagogues [Greek: **the synagogue courts of justice and custody**], and into prisons, being brought before kings and rulers for my name's sake.

"And it shall turn to you for a testimony" (Luke 21:12, 13).

Not only would their words of defense be a testimony for truth, but their unswerving, fearless stedfastness in the face of suffering would speak for itself to all who beheld them.

(2) "And ye shall have tribulation ten days." Most commentators consider that the "ten days" signified that the period of tribulation Jesus was referring to would be limited, or would endure only for a reasonably short term. Satan's power is limited; God's is not! This was a note of encouragement: (a) Their sufferings were not without God's knowledge, notice,

and purpose; and (b) He promised to set a limit on them; they would cease when God's purpose had been accomplished—when they had been sufficiently tried and proven. Considering these assurances, they need not fear their sufferings.

Mortal flesh cringes under suffering, whether it be physical abuse, derision, false accusation with the chagrin of being arrested and jailed, religious persecution, threats, or incessant temptation to do wrong, or compromise, or give up the faith. But there is great strength to be gained from the Scriptures.

Jesus had already felt all that we must feel. He was tempted in all points like as we are, and He did not sin by giving in (Hebrews 4:15). Even He learned obedience to the Father, as the Son of man, by suffering (Hebrews 5:8). We suffer at the hand of a world that hates God, and therefore hates us. But Jesus knew this:

"If the world hate you, ye know that it hated me before it hated you.

"If ye were of the world, the world would love his own: but because ye are not of the world, but I have chosen you out of the world, therefore the world hateth you.

"Remember the word that I said unto you, The servant is not greater than his lord. If they have persecuted me, they will also persecute you; if they have kept my sayings, they will keep yours also.

"But all these things will they do unto you for my name's sake, because they know not him that sent me" (John 15:18-21).

" . . . In the world ye shall have tribulation: but be of good cheer; I have overcome the world" (John 16:33).

As for suffering's limitations, we have the assurance that "There hath no temptation [**testing time** or a **temptation**] taken you but such as is common to man: but God is faithful, who will not suffer you to be tempted [**tested** or **tempted**] above that ye are able; but will with the temptation [**testing time** or **temptation**] also make a way to escape, that ye may be able to bear it" (1 Corinthians 10:13).

Jesus pronounced a blessing upon the persecuted in His "Sermon on the Mount," encouraging rejoicing rather than fear and discouragement (Matthew 5:10-12). To His infant Church He said: "Fear not, little flock; for it is your Father's good pleasure to give you the kingdom" (Luke 12:32). This is in the present tense in the original, for the kingdom of God is ours now, and it is "righteousness, and peace, and joy in the Holy Ghost" (Romans 14:17). We have it already by faith, and it shall be ours forever in eternity.

THE PROMISE TO THE OVERCOMER

" . . . Be thou faithful unto death, and I will give thee a crown of life.

"He that hath an ear, let him hear what the Spirit saith unto the churches; He that overcometh shall not be hurt of the second death" (Revelation 2:10, 11).

As sons of God, there is no security greater than that which He has given us. Some things may **hurt;** they may have to be **endured;** but death for Christ's sake is only an early advance into the fulness of our inheritance.

But we **are** expected to pass the test. Like Job when he was undergoing his great trial, and it seemed that God was far away, he declared: "But he knoweth the way that I take: when he hath tried me, I shall come forth as gold" (Job 23:10; read the whole chapter). Peter heartily agrees with Job's assessment:

"Wherein [in our salvation] ye greatly rejoice, though now for a season, if need be, ye are in heaviness through manifold temptations:

"That the trial of your faith, being much more precious than of gold that perisheth, though it be tried with fire, might be found unto praise and honour and glory at the appearing of Jesus Christ" (1 Peter 1:6, 7).

"Beloved, think it not strange concerning the fiery trial which is to try you, as though some strange thing happened unto you:

"But rejoice, inasmuch as ye are partakers of Christ's sufferings; that, when his glory shall be revealed, ye may be glad also with exceeding joy" (1 Peter 4:12, 13).

Note that Jesus said, in His letter to the saints at Smyrna, "faithful UNTO death," not "UNTIL death." In the context, He was referring to the trials of the saints. If need be, they were to give their lives rather than fail their Lord. It is true that some believers seem never to be subjected to life-threatening trials; however, they may remain faithful throughout a long lifetime, or until death. Of course, they also will receive a crown of life.

It is generally understood that the crown is not a material one, but eternal life itself. James also writes of this crown: "Blessed is the man that endureth temptation [**trial**]: for when he is tried [**has met the test and has been approved**]; he shall receive the crown of life, which the Lord hath promised to them that love him" (James 1:12).

Of course, to receive the crown of life is also to escape "the second death," which is eternity in the lake of fire (Revelation 20:14, 15).

LISTENING TO THE LETTER

The Smyrnians Listened

As was stated earlier, some think that Polycarp was the pastor who received the letter to the church at Smyrna. History does show that he was about that time the "bishop of the church at Smyrna," and that he was martyred there, without the sanction of the Roman government, about A.D. 155. The order for his execution was given by the Proconsul of Asia Minor, "who demanded that Polycarp swear by the genius of Caesar and renounce Christ" (**Schaff's History of the Christian Church,** Vol. II, page 760). He was "faithful unto death," refusing to deny His Saviour, and was burned at the stake at the age of eighty-six years. One account states that the Jews helped bring the wood to feed the flames!

Polycarp listened to the letter, either at the time it was received, or at a later date. He purposed in his heart to stand the test, though it did not come for many years.

Again, imagine this congregation giving close attention to every word as the letter from Christ, by John's hand, was read to them. Hearing no word of reproof, they must have felt gratefully humbled at their Saviour's appraisal.

Of course, they were already acquainted with the afflictions of tribulation and poverty, so they may have felt blessed to be chosen to further suffer shame for His name, as did the apostles when they were beaten and threatened at Jerusalem early in their ministry (Acts 5:40, 41). Having been faithful thus far, they would surely cast all fear aside and continue pressing toward the mark laid out for the overcomer. As Paul had said, they would "fight the good fight of faith, [and] lay hold on eternal life" (1 Timothy 6:12). No matter how severe the tribulation, it would be limited by the will of God. They could take it; and they must, for His name's sake.

Are WE Listening?

If our local church should be commended as the church at Smyrna was, what would be our reaction? Would we be exalted, or would we be humbled? Would we ask, "Why the sufferings when our works are pleasing to God?" Or would we pray, "O Lord, through our sufferings, help us to be strengthened to our resolve to gain the crown of life"?

We are living in a time when "evil men and seducers shall wax worse and worse, deceiving and being deceived" (2 Timothy 3:13). Therefore, we must brace ourselves for whatever comes, in whatever form. When hurricanes and tornadoes strike, we have no power over the storm, but we can pray and do whatever seems wise to keep from being killed. All of our possessions may be swept away, but the storms cannot touch our souls—unless we become embittered over our losses.

Men have learned to make long-term preparations against earthquakes, floods, drouths, and fire, by building so that their power of destruction is diminished or minimized; but the principal guarantee is to have everything so completely committed to Christ, and to God's will, that even the worst won't disturb our peace of mind and soul. Being prepared alleviates our fears. Jesus said, "Fear none of those things which thou shalt suffer." We may fear circumstances—the possibility of adversity—evil personalities. We may fear being criticized if we speak the truth boldly and plainly. We may fear Satan. But Jesus has told us what to fear:

> "And I say unto you my friends, Be not afraid of them that kill the body, and after that have no more that they can do.
>
> "But I will forewarn you whom ye shall fear: Fear

him, which after he hath killed hath power to cast into hell; yea, I say unto you, Fear him.
"Are not five sparrows sold for two farthings, and not one of them is forgotten before God?
"But even the very hairs of your head are all numbered. Fear not therefore: ye are of more value than many sparrows" (Luke 12:4-7).

If we fear God, we have no reason to fear the devil, for Jesus came to destroy him and his wicked works (Hebrews 2:14; 1 John 3:8). He has no power over the blood-bought children of God unless we submit to his temptations from without. The Apostle Paul knew he would face suffering—"bonds [imprisonment] and afflictions"—but this did not disturb him (Acts 20:22-24), for he knew something much greater. As a Roman prisoner for defending the gospel, he rather encouraged Timothy, his fellowminister, with these words:

> "For the which cause [the gospel] I also suffer these things: nevertheless I am not ashamed: for I know whom I have believed, and am persuaded that he is able to keep that which I have committed unto him against that day" (2 Timothy 1:12).

We have a God-given desire to live, but beyond that we have a God-given promise of eternal life—a place prepared for us where the adverse conditions we are familiar with in this life will forevermore be absent.

Will your pastor and mine, your local church and mine, give heed to what the Spirit is saying to the Church of God today through this brief letter to the church at Smyrna? If not, will you and I as individual members be found overcomers, coming forth in the first resurrection, untouched by "the second death"? We will if the purpose of our hearts is to "fear not," and to "be faithful unto death."

LORD, BE IT SO!

—Lesson Five—

THE CHURCH AT PERGAMOS

RELATION OF THE CITY AND CHURCH

Geographical, Cultural, and Historical Situation

Geography: Pergamos (Pergamum) was an inland city, situated in the district of Mysia on the Caicus River. It was about fifty miles north of Smyrna. Because of its interior setting, it was not as noted as Ephesus and Smyrna for trade, but it excelled them historically and politically.

Culture and History: The beginning of Pergamos is unknown, but it predates the Greek period. It has been designated as "an outpost of Greek civilization"—its sculpture and architecture, and the worship of Greek gods: Zeus, Athena, Apollo, Aesculapius, Dionysus, Aphrodite, and later Augustus [Caesar] and Trajan. Zeus was the supreme deity of the ancient Greeks, the father of gods and men, and all their activities. The highest achievement of Greek sculpture was said to have been his statue at Olympia.

Corrupt morals prevailed, associated with the many idols. Morally contaminating idolatrous rites were frequent and varied. Aesculapius was the patron divinity of medicine, and it is said that his name meant "Savior." His idol was in the form of a serpent. The touch of the tame snakes which were loose in this temple was thought to bring health and healing. Those seeking healing might spend the night in the dark temple, hoping for the serpent's touch.

There was a university at Pergamos, and at one time there was a library of two hundred thousand volumes. Pergamos is credited with the development of parchment (pergamenos), a paper made from the skins of animals "to free the library from Egypt's jealous ban on the export of papyrus" (**Zondervan's Bible Dictionary**).

The **Thompson Bible Survey** says: "History does not record the origin of the Christian faith in Pergamos, but the church was probably founded by Paul, who was in the general area on his missionary journeys. Apparently the church became well established about thirty years later . . . John's transmitting of the letter to the believers at Pergamos suggests that he had ministered in their midst." Again, it seems likely that Pergamos would have had a place in Acts if Paul had worked there. It is more probable that he inspired some other minister to carry the gospel into that area.

Pergamos is mentioned in the Bible only in Revelation. Later history records much persecution and many martyrdoms.

Pergamos is now the modern Bergama, which is much smaller, and without the former glory. The **Thompson Bible Survey** states: "Little Christian witness is now evident in this once great Christian city."

CHRIST INTRODUCES HIMSELF

"And to the angel of the church in Pergamos write; These things saith he which hath the sharp sword with two edges" (Revelation 2:12).

The Two-edged Sword

Already, in chapter 1, verse 16, John had seen Christ in a similar light—". . . out of his mouth went a sharp twoedged sword." We have noted this briefly in Lesson Two.

Here, Christ identified Himself as the One who had the sharp sword with two edges. It seems safe to assume that the two references belong together, and that the sword proceeds from His mouth. This indicates that, basically, the sword signifies the Word of God, whether in the mouth or the hand, and whether wielded by Christ, the Holy Ghost, or holy men who are moved upon and used by him. Some other scriptural witnesses to this application are as follows:

"In the beginning was the Word, and the Word was with God, and the Word was God . . . .
"And the Word was made flesh, and dwelt among us [in the person of Christ]" (John 1:1, 14).

"And take . . . the sword of the Spirit, which is the word of God" (Ephesians 6:17).

"Let the high praises of God be in their [the saints'] mouth, and a twoedged sword in their hand" (Psalms 149:6).

"And then shall that Wicked [the Antichrist] be revealed, whom the Lord shall consume with the spirit of his mouth . . . " (2 Thessalonians 2:8).

"And out of his [Christ's] mouth goeth a sharp sword, that with it he should smite the nations . . . .
"And the remnant were slain with the sword of him that sat upon the horse, which sword proceeded out of his mouth" (Revelation 19:15, 21).

The Word of God is the Word of a loving God, and of a just God. Like God Himself, it is no respecter of persons. The individual's reaction to the declared Word determines which way it will cut. It can be either a great binder or a great divider.

According to Hebrews 4:12, it is "quick" (living and operative); it is "powerful" (energetic and authoritative). It is sharp—piercing—penetrating. It goes into the depths, "dividing asunder" as it goes, discerning or bringing to light the very secret thoughts and intentions of the heart. It separates, divides, or distinguishes the right from the wrong, the truth from error, the facts from deception.

It is noteworthy that Hebrews 4:13 continues reference to the Word of God, but personifies it: "Neither is there any creature that is not manifest in HIS [Christ, the Word's] sight: but all things are naked and opened unto the eyes of him with whom we have to do."

What an introduction of Himself this must have been to the pastor and congregation at Pergamos! No doubt they were already thinking of those things among them (verses 14 and 15) that were "naked and opened unto the eyes" of this mighty One who not only "hath the sharp sword," but WAS (and IS) that sword!

Numerous suggestions have been offered as to the meaning of the two "edges": (a) The Law and the Gospel, or law and grace; (b) mercy and judgment; (c) healing and wounding; (d) blessing and condemnation; (e) persuasion and compulsion; (f) tender pleading and unbending authority. In each and all of these "two-edged" speculations we can clearly discern the mighty Christ of God as the fulfiller or personifier. He had the power and authority to bestow approval (grace) where approval was due, and to mete out judgment (law) where the sinner would not honor the eternal Word. **Adam Clarke** has well said: "Jesus has the sword with the two edges, because

He is the Saviour of sinners, and the Judge of [both] the quick [the living] and the dead." The Word of God is no idle Word. It is active. What proceeds from the MOUTH of God is carried out by the HAND of God.

CHRIST'S APPRAISAL OF THE CHURCH

"I know thy works and where thou dwellest, even where Satan's seat is: and thou holdest fast my name, and hast not denied my faith, even in those days wherein Antipas was my faithful martyr, who was slain among you, where Satan dwelleth" (Revelation 2:13).

Observations and Commendations

Observations: He knew (a) their works, and (b) where they dwelt, "even where Satan's seat [throne] is." As to their works, some were commendable and some were reprovable, as we shall see.

He knew their municipal environment, seething with satanic influences. "Satan's seat" and "where Satan dwelleth" refer to the satanic power resident in the evil "religious" character of the city. This was evident in their persecution of Christians, and was perhaps represented in their worship of Aesculapius, the serpent god.

Satan's "throne," or dwelling place, may have referred to "a cluster of temples" in Pergamos that had been erected in honor of the idol gods named under "Culture and History" in this lesson. These temples were situated as a sort of complex in "a beautiful grove called Nicephorium, the pride of Pergamum. It is possible that the mention of Satan points to the serpent, which was so prominent in the cult of Aesculapius.

Matthew Henry notes that "the Roman governor in this city was a most violent enemy of the Christians; and the seat of persecutions in Satan's seat."

Though opinions vary slightly, one thing is certain: Satan, the prince of this world, enthrones himself, and is worshipped in varying degrees, in every city, town, village, and community on earth. Every local church must function in the midst of this opposing power. Every member must understand this, and be determined to cope with it without compromise.

Commendations: The church at Pergamos (a) was holding

fast Christ's name, and (b) they had not denied the faith, even when one of their own number had been slain and they had reason to think that they might all suffer the same. Though this church had some serious faults, to say the least, the merciful justice of God did not discount the stedfastness of the faithful ones—which may have been the majority.

Christ commended them for honoring His name. Recall again His rebuke of those who claimed to do "many wonderful works" in His name, but were deceivers (Matthew 7:22, 23). At Pergamos, it was different, and He knew the difference. It is one thing to honor Jesus' name by reverent recognition of His God-given power and authority, never forgetting that we are saved and kept by His merits, not our own. It is another thing to mouth His name for personal advantage or prestige. Even the devils know the difference, as is seen in that instance where some vagabond Jewish exorcists (casters-out-of-devils) took it upon themselves to say to the evil spirits, "We adjure you by Jesus whom Paul preacheth." (Read Acts 19:13-16.)

Jesus had said that if Satan should cast out Satan, he would be divided against himself, and his kingdom would fall (Matthew 12:26). Those devils in Acts 19 knew both Jesus and Paul, and beyond that, they knew that this deceiver had no power over them simply by using the "Name" of Him who has all power in heaven and in earth. It is commendable to use His name only when such is done legitimately.

Christ commended this church for not denying His faith, or their faith in Him as their only Deliverer and Lord. In this context, there is only "one faith" (Ephesians 4:15), "the faith which was once delivered unto the saints" (Jude 3). Greek Expositor **Kenneth S. Wuest** says the Greek word for "once" means "once for all," indicating that no other faith will be given. This is another scriptural witness that there is only one faith; and it was this faith which the saints at Pergamos had kept, or had not denied.

The reference to the martyrdom of one named Antipas infers that he died for that one faith, and that his death had not weakened, through fear, the faith of the remaining saints. Nothing more is known about Antipas than that Jesus adjudged him His "faithful martyr." But, after all, what more need be said of any mortal? And will not heaven reveal thousands of redeemed souls of whom nothing more is known among men than the glorious fact that they did not deny the faith? If so, they share the same heaven with the illustrious Apostle Paul, who declared that he had "kept the faith" and, therefore, felt assured that "a crown of righteousness" awaited him (2 Timothy 4:7, 8).

The Indictments

> "But I have a few things against thee, because thou hast them that hold the doctrine of Balaam, who taught Balac to cast a stumblingblock before the children of Israel, to eat things sacrificed unto idols, and to commit fornication.
> "So hast thou also them that hold the doctrine of the Nicolaitans, which thing I hate" (Revelation 2:14, 15).

This church had some highly commendable attributes in its favor, but Jesus said, "I have a few things against thee." It is not the number of things that count, either for us or against us. The magnitude of those things is what matters. In this case, the two major indictments were such that the "sword" of judgment was about to fall upon this compromising church.

The Doctrine of Balaam: This false doctrine is too important to pass over lightly, but at least, we can give the gist of it here in its several applications.

For a beginning, it will be helpful—perhaps necessary—for the student to read Numbers, chapters 22 through 25, and chapter 31, verses 1 through 24; also 2 Peter, chapter 2, and Jude in its entirety. In both of these New Testament references the context is false prophets and their apostate teachings. These advance readings will make our abbreviated treatment of the subject more intelligible. (NOTE: The tract, "Try The Spirits" (false teachings booklet), by **A. J. Tomlinson,** conveys some interesting thoughts for our day and time.)

Balaam was a prophet (2 Peter 2:16). Some brand him as "a typical hireling prophet." Others consider him to have once been a prophet of the true God, but had himself taken up sorcery and divination, more or less "juggling" the two "ministries." **Matthew Henry** supposes him to have been "a famous conjurer [magician; sorcerer]," who was called upon by kings (such as Balak) to throw light on their problems. At any rate, Balaam's association with divination, soothsaying, enchantments, and the like, is evidenced from Numbers 22:7, Numbers 24:1, and Joshua 13:22.

As to the reason for, and the nature of, the communication between God and Balaam, some commentators do not so much as venture a speculation. Others go to great complicated and confusing lengths. **Henry** offers what seems to be a sensible suggestion: "God sometimes, for the preservation of His people, was pleased to speak to bad men." It is of no profit to wrestle with issues which our sovereign God, who does all things well, has chosen to leave obscure.

We know that God spoke with Balaam; He counselled Balaam; He rebuked Balaam. In fact, God **used** Balaam; first, in bringing about a well-deserved, severe chastening plague upon His chosen people, which was ultimately for their good; second, in spreading a somber warning on the pages of Holy Writ for all succeeding generations. This is seen in the fact that Christ was recalling it as an admonition to His Church some sixteen centuries after the initial episode. Furthermore, Christ's personal appraisal of the matter in His letter to Pergamos is the ultimate identification of the character of this "doctrine of Balaam."

(1) **The Stumbling Block Characteristic:** A stumbling block is an obstruction or obstacle so situated that, because of its obscurity, it is not seen or noticed by those whom it is intended to deceive, or injure, or ensnare. It may be designed with sideline attractions to divert attention from the principal object. In this sense it is deceptive, its main purpose being to lead one on.

In the case of Balaam's doctrine, the stumbling block was its "religious" characteristic. Since it is basically evil, it will adapt itself to appeal to the individual, or the group, or the particular church which it hopes to deceive. Very likely it will introduce itself through the mode of worship, in this way gaining the confidence of the worshipper. The pastor and saints at Pergamos were being plagued by some sort of rational deception with which God was greatly displeased.

It is not unusual for the real perpetrator to stay in the background, as Balaam used (taught) King Balak to lay the stumbling block and promote the doctrine.

(2) **The Idol Fellowship Characteristic:** The stumbling block subtly merged itself into this second characteristic,

"religiously," possibly in the name of "fellowship," declaring it "no harm" to eat things sacrificed unto idols. There can be little doubt that the church at Pergamos was familiar with the decree that had been delivered to the churches after the council at Jerusalem—"that ye abstain from meats offered to idols" (Acts 15:29).

It is also possible that the Balaamites imposed their "private interpretation" onto Paul's exposition on meats and drinks (Romans 14 and 1 Corinthians 8). This church was in a city that was engulfed in idolatry, and the members were in all probability converts from the cults which held idol feasts. A compromise on this point might have afforded the more "social favor" and less persecution.

(3) **The Fornication Characteristic:** The "stumbling" effect continued. It was an easy "blunder" from social fellowship to fornication, which was undoubtedly the design of the deceivers from the outset.

In the context of this problem as it existed at Pergamos, "fornication" must be understood in its total concept. **Webster's** classical definition is as follows: "Voluntary sexual intercourse between an unmarried woman and man, especially an unmarried man [1 Corinthians 5:1]. In the Bible, (a) any unlawful sexual intercourse, including adultery; (b) worship of idols [sometimes called spiritual adultery]." In the light of the Scriptures rightly divided, **Webster's** definition must be modified somewhat. Fornication always involves at least one single person. This is still true with fornication in marriage relationships; that is, one who has never been lawfully married or who is free to marry because of the death of a legitimate companion. In an illicit marriage involving one single person and another who is lawfully married (has a living companion, though divorced), the single person is the fornicator and the married one is an adulterer or adulteress. Any form of double marriage is sinful.

During his years of earth-ministry, Jesus made three things clear concerning divorce and remarriage: (1) Divorce of lawfully married couples is a violation of the will and commandment of God (Matthew 5:31, 32); (2) divorce opens the way for and encourages adulterous acts and marriages (Matthew 19:3-9); and (3) there is only one exception to the "no divorce" implication of God's covenant stipulation, "Let not man put asunder"—that is, a single person who is married to one with a living lawful companion, should divorce because the single person is a fornicator and the divorced person is an adulterer or adulteress, making an unlawful marriage. They are in a state of fornication and living in adultery. The single person is free to marry another single companion since he or she has never had a lawful companion. Jesus therefore declared "the cause of fornication" to be the only exception to His "no divorce" commandment.

The fornication at Pergamos probably involved all forms of adulterous sin, since these were actually a part of most pagan religion. The original design was to bring a curse on God's people. Fornication and intermarriage would be sinful in themselves, but they would also lead to **Webster's** second definition—"worship of idols." This was an oft-repeated sin in Israel, and it is reasonable to believe that the doctrine of Balaam was at the root of this abomination. Numbers, chapter 25, seems to be the first instance of this adulterous idolatry of Israel on a national scale. Jesus' words to Pergamos are heaven's authentication of the real meaning of the entire matter.

Any recognition or worship of other gods was a violation of God's First Commandment. He is a jealous God (Exodus 20:5; 34:14; Deuteronomy 4:24; 5:9; 6:14, 15), and He is both grieved and angered when His people allow themselves to be led away from His truth. It was compromise, and God would have none of it. Compromise says, "We'll go part way with you if you'll go part way with us." It is a mixture of TRUTH AND ERROR—the holy standard of God and the unholy practices of paganism. It rears its ugly head in various forms: mixing law and grace; the secular social amenities with the fellowship of the saints; the excesses of this world with the separated life in Christ. In Paul's words, it is an unequal yoke:

> "Be ye not unequally yoked together with unbelievers: for what fellowship hath righteousness with unrighteousness? and what communion hath light with darkness?
>
> "And what concord hath Christ with Belial? or what part hath he that believeth with an infidel?
>
> "And what agreement hath the temple of God with idols? for ye are the temple of the living God, as God hath said, I will dwell in them, and walk in them; and I

will be their God, and they shall be my people.

"Wherefore come out from among them, and be ye separate, saith the Lord, and touch not the unclean thing; and I will receive you,

"And will be a Father unto you, and ye shall be my sons and daughters, saith the Lord Almighty" (2 Corinthians 6:14-18).

It is clear that the promises are conditional upon the separations.

The Covetousness Characteristic: This characteristic of the doctrine of Balaam is seen in 2 Peter 2:15, where love for "the wages of unrighteousness" is designated as "the way of Balaam." In the original episode, Balak offered a reward if Balaam would curse Israel. Apparently the amount of the reward was increased from time to time (Numbers 23:10-13), and, though Balaam feared God enough that he dared not curse Israel, his persistence in going back to God again and again shows that in his heart he loved the reward and wanted it. In the end, he did not curse Israel, but he devised a scheme whereby they would bring the curse upon themselves. Is it too much to assume that, somewhere along the way, Balak gave him his "wages"?

It has been suggested that Jude's mention of "the error of Balaam" refers to the eventual destruction which will befall the false teachers, just as Balaam's erroneous thinking finally led to his death at the hands of those he endeavored to curse (Numbers 31:8).

The Doctrine of the Nicolaitanes: This doctrine was examined in Lesson Three, under "One Final Commendation" for the church at Ephesus. The commendation was, "thou hatest the deeds of the Nicolaitanes, which I also hate." (Review that section of Lesson Three.)

To the church at Pergamos, Jesus spoke of "the doctrine of the Nicolaitanes, which thing I hate." The reference is virtually the same, since their "deeds" were simply their "doctrine" in action.

Putting it simply, "the doctrine of the Nicolaitanes" was a love for "the world, [and] the things that are in the world" (1 John 2:15, 16), to the extent that they tried to justify it by a false interpretation of "grace." It was a misplaced love, and therefore hateful to God.

Christianity has been plagued by this doctrine in almost every generation, even though it has not often been identified by name. Wherever, and whenever, the biblical doctrine of sanctification is neglected, or taught only as a gradual process (which is seldom pursued voluntarily), the world has a heyday. Unrestricted "freedom" is claimed as a "right," but it is actually nothing more than an even more deadly form of bondage, for it deceives and destroys in the name of "Christian liberty." Since the individual who holds this doctrine is lacking in experiential grace, he seldom responds positively to the doctrine of the separated life of holiness; however, he lays claim to it. This is Nicolaitanism.

Summarily, the indictment for both of these false doctrines lies in the fact that either the pastor or certain members of this church were allowed to "hold" these beliefs, apparently unreproved. Soon this "leaven" would defile "the whole lump" (1 Corinthians 5:6; Galatians 5:9). Did the pastor not care? Were the unaffected ones so unconcerned? It was clearly a matter for concern with Christ. In a word, He knew these things, and He was holding it against them.

ADMONITION, EXHORTATION, AND CONSEQUENCES

"Repent; or else I will come unto thee quickly, and will fight against them with the sword of my mouth" (Revelation 2:16).

The Charge

"**Repent...**" Wherever there is wrongdoing, God requires repentance to the point of godly sorrow and turning away from the thing to be repented of.

If the pastor at Pergamos was guilty of involvement in Balaamism of Nicolaitanism, or even of being sympathetic with those who "held" those destructive doctrines, he must repent. If either the church or pastor was derelict in their duty to stand up against those who were mixing their sinful "leaven" with the truth, the pastor and/or the church must repent and shoulder their responsibility. It has been said, "Those who sin together should repent together....When God comes to punish the corrupt members of a church, He rebukes that church itself for allowing such to continue in the communion."

When Simon, the sorcerer in Samaria, professed to believe the gospel preached by Philip, yet tried to purchase the gift of the Holy Ghost with money, the Apostle Peter rebuked him sharply, telling him that his heart was not right in the sight of God. His "believing" was intellectual only, and it did not save. Peter's admonition was: "Repent therefore of this thy wickedness, and pray God, if perhaps the thought of thine heart may be forgiven thee" (Acts 8:22).

The prophets of old repeatedly pled with Israel to "turn" or "return to" the Lord when they had sinned against Him. In other words, they were to repent, then prove it by turning away from their sin unto the Lord. (See Hosea 14:1, 2; Joel 2:13; also 1 Kings 8:33-36; Psalms 7:11-13; and Proverbs 1:22-29.)

The Consequences

Divine Judgment: It would come "quickly," or suddenly and surprisingly. He who fights or wars against God is destined to lose. To resist His Word of warning is to invite sure disaster. The power of God's Word is awesome. The worlds were "framed"—planned and brought into existence—by the Word of God (Hebrews 11:3; Colossians 1:16), and all things are upheld (sustained, operated, guided) "by the word of his power" (Hebrews 1:3). In the beginning, "God said, Let . . . ," and it was done (Genesis 1:3, 9, 11, 14, 24, 26)!

Who would dare to resist His Word? Who would presume to engage in battle with "the sword of [His] mouth"? The prophet Isaiah has recorded it thus:

> "If ye be willing and obedient, ye shall eat the good of the land:
> "But if ye refuse and rebel, ye shall be devoured with the sword: for the mouth of the Lord hath spoken it" (Isaiah 1:19, 20).

The church at Pergamos was being challenged by an invincible power. It was "Repent; or else"! It was either deal with those advocates of false doctrines or else subject themselves to the sure judgment of God. What would they do?

THE PROMISE TO THE OVERCOMER

"He that hath an ear, let him hear what the Spirit

saith unto the churches; To him that overcometh will I give to eat of the hidden manna, and will give him a white stone, and in the stone a new name written, which no man knoweth saving he that receiveth it" (Revelation 2:17).

Jesus spoke, then left the verdict with them. The guilty ones were free moral agents; they could either repent or persist in their own way. As a rule, when wrongdoing once gains a foothold, the righteous element feels that "their hands are tied"—that they will be silenced for "causing dissension." But "peace at any price" is not peace. It is compromise.

In this late Twentieth Century, in society as a whole, the real culprit's so-called "rights" are ridiculously protected while the innocent ones become the victims. When a church entertains this position, the "leaven" spreads so rapidly that sin declares itself to be "the norm." But God's Word is the true norm; and the individual overcomer has His promise of reward. For the Pergamos saints, the reward was three-fold:

(1) **The "hidden manna":** While the heretics were feasting on idolatry and fornication, the overcomers would be given "bread from heaven." It is "hidden" in the sense that Christ, the true bread of life, is not really "seen" through the sinful eye, neither is He "known" by the corrupt mind: "Whosoever sinneth hath not SEEN him, neither KNOWN him" (1 John 3:6). Even the true "sons of God" now see Him "through a glass, darkly," but in the time of perfection, we shall see Him face to face (1 Corinthians 13:12). John says it in these words:

> "Beloved, now are we the sons of God, and it doth not yet appear what we shall be: but we know that, when he shall appear, we shall be like him; for we shall see him as he is" (1 John 3:2).

(2) **A "white stone":** It is commonly agreed that the bestowal of a white stone to the overcomer was a spiritual figure derived from an ancient practice in courts of justice; a black stone was given to the one condemned, but a white stone was bestowed upon the one acquitted.

"Therefore being justified [acquitted] by faith, we have

peace with God through our Lord Jesus Christ: "By whom also we have access by faith into this grace [of justification, or acquittal] wherein we stand, and rejoice in hope of the glory of God" (Romans 5:1, 2).

This acquittal is ours "by faith." We await the final "glorification" stage—"in hope of the glory of God" and if we are overcomers in the end, we will receive the white stone.

(3) **A "new name":** This is something of a mystery. However, we are reminded of the ancient biblical practice of name-changing when names had a meaning that related to the individual's attributes or character. For instance, "Abram" meant **high father;** "Abraham" meant **father of many nations.** "Sarai" meant **contentious;** "Sarah" meant **princess.** "Saul" meant **asked for,** a Hebrew name; "Paul" meant **little** in Latin, or Roman, but **extraordinary** or **wonderful** in Hebrew. "Simon" meant a **hearkening;** both "Peter" and "Cephas" (John 1:42) meant **a stone** (petros, a stone, or **small piece of petra,** a rock).

Paul says, "... If any man be in Christ [saved, or justified], he is a new creature: old things are passed away; behold, all things are become new" (2 Corinthians 5:17). His relationship with God is changed. Who knows what name God might use if He were conversing orally and verbally with us as redeemed individuals? We do not know now, but apparently we shall know in His own time.

It has been suggested that the new name is the name of adoption, whereby we are given the name of the family of God, into which we have been received—"accepted in [Christ] the beloved" (Ephesians 1:6)—and made "children, joint-heirs with Christ" (Romans 8:17). Some have gone so far as to say that the name on every overcomer's white stone will be Christ's name. Be that as it may, it is a beautiful thought; and surely every blood-bought believer would humbly rejoice to bear His dear name.

LISTENING TO THE LETTER

Pergamos Listened

What must have been the surprised reaction when the pastor received a letter, thinking it was from the Apostle John, then to read the salutation, "These things saith he which hath the sharp sword with two edges"? Certainly, if he had had any access to the Scriptures at all, he knew immediately that Christ alone answered to that introduction.

Then, imagine the excitement—perhaps mingled with dread and fear in some quarters—when the members were notified that a letter from Christ had just been received, and would be read in their hearing at a specified time! There may have been some skepticism as to its authenticity, but curiosity alone probably impelled them to come to the reading.

Yes, they had heard of the two-edged sword, typifying the powerful, piercing, soul-searching, convicting Word of God. The faithful element was undoubtedly thrilled to hear those opening words, for it had been the consecrated purpose of their hearts to know more about that Word, and to live by its every jot and tittle.

But is it not true that every man who holds to his private opinions, yet declaring "special revelation from God," knows in his heart that he is wrong? Those who held "the doctrine of Balaam" did so despite their having heard the truth. They almost certainly knew that their views were in flagrant violation of the First and Second Commandments of God's unchanging moral law. And, to be "Christian" at all, they had to know that fornication, either fleshly or spiritual, was a reproach to the Christ to whom they gave lip-service.

What were their thoughts when He announced, "I know thy works"? Did they flinch when "Satan's seat" and his dwelling place were cited? Or were their hearts already hardened to the point where they could join the faithful ones in their "Amens"? Were their hearts stung even slightly at the mention of Christ's faithful martyr Antipas, whom they may have—secretly, of course!—turned over to his slayers, for "the wages of unrighteousness," Judas fashion?

Then, the worldly Nicolaitanes and their loose doctrine—yes, they were listening. Were they, too, pretentiously joining in the "Amens" of the stedfast number, or were they seething inwardly with disdain and anger? Did they even care that Jesus hated their doctrine?

Of course, we are not told what the response was to Jesus' admonition to repent, and the consequences to be expected if they refused. Did the pastor weep with remorse of soul, in case he had failed, or refused, to discipline the apostates? Did he feel chastened by the Spirit of grace, in case he himself had "leanings" in the wrong direction?

What about the followers of those who had spread this satanic leaven among them? Perhaps they were awakened to the deceptive spirit that had them under its influence. Perhaps they cried out to God for mercy and forgiveness. But we know that Satan is not easily dethroned. It is altogether likely that some had already been deluded to "the point of no return"! Is it not usually so?

Are WE Listening?

Is "Jesus Christ the same yesterday, and today, and for ever" addressing the Church today through this letter which has been included in the inspired canons that make up the Bible? Since it was addressed to "the angel of the church in Pergamos," it is easy to "leave it with Pergamos." In fact, it has been treated thus down through the ages of Christendom. The fact that Balaamism and Nicolaitanism are not extinct testifies that this letter has been largely disregarded.

Do we hear the resounding indictments? Do we even ask ourselves if these two evil doctrines are possibly "leavening our meal," but under "religious" names?

Idolatry is idolatry, regardless of the "sheep's clothing" it wears. Since **covetousness** is idolatry, its undergarment is still "the wages of unrighteousness" which many love to wear while they tout the popular "success philosophy"!

Self-exaltation seems to have a wide-open field in many churches—"all to the glory of God," they say! Its root is "secular humanism." Its cloak is misnomered "Christian psychology." He whose "name shall be called Wonderful, Counsellor" (Isaiah 9:6) is being scuttled "to the back seat" or "under my footstool" in some areas, while the wearers of "the gay clothing" of wealth, prestige, kinship, and higher education are lavishly introduced with "respect of person." (Read James 2:1-4.)

Are we listening to Jesus' indictment of **worldliness,** even though it has long since discarded its early title of "Nicolaitanism"? In today's "everything goes," permissive society, "worldliness" has been defined and redefined—as though it were being "refined"; but it would seem that the skimmings of scum and dregs have been mistaken for the pure silver in the refining pot!

But Jesus still says, "WHICH THING I HATE"!

He apparently knew that it would have been profitless to elaborate—to describe "worldliness" and its attendant low morals to the church at Pergamos. He knew that they knew what the Scriptures mean by "the world, and the things that are in the world." It would have been pointless to waste words. He simply pronounced the indictment and left it with them to be honest or dishonest with their own hearts.

Now, He leaves it to us to listen to the same message. And He need not elaborate, for He knows that we know what "worldliness" is. He is not mocked. He does not pander to men's redefinitions. The two-edged sword of God's Word, which is "settled in heaven" (Psalms 119:89), is in His hand. All who should repent but refuse to do so stand judged by the sword of His mouth. We may argue, if we will. We may lie to our own hearts, and go our own way in the name of "freedom." Free-will allows us our choice. But if we have ears, let us hear what the Spirit is saying to the Church today.

The overcomers have nothing to fear from His indictments. The rewards are waiting. But God grant that we do not forget that the finish line still lies beyond us. And God help us to endure to the end!

—Lesson Six—
THE CHURCH AT THYATIRA
RELATION OF CITY AND CHURCH

Geographical, Cultural, and Historical Situation

Geography: Thyatira was a relatively obscure city forty miles southeast of Pergamos, on the border between the districts of Lydia and Mysia. It was on a caravan road between the Hermus and Caicus Rivers. This highway led to Sardis fifty miles to the south.

Thyatira was in a rich agricultural area and was a city of commerce, including wool and linen workers, garment makers, leather workers, potters and bronze-smiths. It was famous for the making of purple dye, the color of the raiment of kings and dignitaries. Reference is made in Acts 16:14 to "a certain woman named Lydia, a seller of purple, of the city of Thyatira." At the time, she was in Macedonian Philippi when Paul established the church there.

History mentions the many trade guilds which influenced, and even controlled, commerce to a great extent. These guilds were an early "distant relative" of today's trade unions. The success of one's business depended greatly upon membership in the guild. In fact, participation in the city's social life was almost mandatory for guild members.

Culture and History: Thyatira's early history is meager and by no means illustrious. It was a border outpost known both as Pelopia and Auhippa around 280 B.C. when one of the generals of Alexander the Great colonized it with Greeks from Macedonia, and changed the name to Thyatira. This probably accounts for Lydia having been in Macedonia selling purple dye (and perhaps textiles) in Paul's time.

Temples in Thyatira were dedicated to Apollo, the sun god, and Artemis (the Ephesian Diana), but there was no temple to the Roman Emperor. The church may have been established by one of Paul's associates, but more likely by the influence of Lydia. Christ's letter, written by John's hand, was sent to Thyatira more than 40 years after Paul had met Lydia at Philippi, but it is not known just when the church was established. Seemingly it was a small church, but Christ deemed it important enough to be included in His revelation.

It is said that there is a Moslim mosque on the site of the former church at Thyatira.

Early Thyatira is today's modern Turkish Akhisar, with a population of about 50,000. There are a few Christians living there.

CHRIST INTRODUCES HIMSELF

> "And unto the angel of the church in Thyatira write; These things saith the Son of God, who hath his eyes like unto a flame of fire, and his feet are like fine brass" (Revelation 2:18).

God the Son

Jesus forthrightly declared Himself to be the Son of God as the correspondent. This probably had two meanings, for there were both an ungodly and a godly people there. To the godly it meant a majestic and glorious Presence in written form; a visitation of love and care. To the ungodly it was a solemn reminder of the unmitigated power of judgment; perhaps of impending judgment that could fall at any moment. It was a message from the Father of glory through the person of the Son.

This church, or its pastor, was entertaining an evil influence, as we shall see. The spirit of worship had to be corrupt and devoid of unity. This called for nothing short of an abrupt reminder of the mighty Deity resident in the Christ by whom they had been saved. It would have been a callous heart and mind indeed that would not have been shaken by so personal a salutation.

Flaming Eyes

The "eyes like unto a flame of fire" bespoke His omniscience; His awareness of even the hidden intents of every heart. They burned with holy indignation and purging judgment against all wickedness, yet at the same time with fervent love toward those whom He would immediately commend.

Feet of Fine Brass

This declared the refined purity with which He walked, as well as the fiery judgment which brass always betokens in the Scriptures. They were the feet of Him who had said, while they still walked this earth:

"... The Father judgeth no man, but hath committed all judgment unto the Son: That all men should honour the Son, even as they honour the Father ... " (John 5:22, 23).

The feet that were pierced on Calvary were now proclaimed to be walking in Thyatira, trampling down the unholy doctrines He knew were being taught there, yet making a highway for the pure and clean to travel on (Isaiah 35:8):

CHRIST'S APPRAISAL OF THE CHURCH

"I know thy works, and charity, and service, and faith, and thy patience, and thy works; and the last [works] to be more than the first" (Revelation 2:19).

Commendations

The omniscient Christ makes no errors in judgment, or appraisal. He KNOWS. He knew the good works that were being done in Thyatira; and He knew the reprehensible works also. But, as with all the churches, He first commended them.

(1) **He knew their charity:** It is noteworthy that no other church was commended for its charity, or love. Others no doubt had some measure of love, but this was one of Thyatira's strong points in the Saviour's flaming eyes. Charity generally means "love in action." John describes it simply and practically:

"My little children, let us not love in word, neither in tongue [only]; but in deed [practical works] and in truth [according to truth]" (1 John 3:18).

This includes "all men," as well as "the brethren"—or fellow-Christians. One may be able to quote many verses of Scripture on love, and to preach well on the subject, yet do none of those things which administer that love to those who feel neglected, forsaken, and unloved.

(2) **He knew their service:** This substantiated their charity, as John advocates. It is probable that this church was noted in the city for its care for the poor, for widows and orphans, and for lending a helping hand in times of disaster, misfortune, sickness, and other incapacities. In Jesus' searching eyes, this was praiseworthy, though it could not save.

(3) **He knew their faith:** Faith, charity, and service complement each other, both practically and spiritually. As unshakable faith, or unwavering belief in God's Word, translates into a love that serves both God and humanity. "Now faith is the SUBSTANCE of things hoped for, the EVIDENCE of things not seen" (Hebrews 11:1). In other words, faith brings to reality things that would otherwise be empty and unproductive. James approaches John's premise, cited above, from the stance of faith:

"What doth it profit, my brethren, though a man say he hath faith, and have not works? can faith save him?

"If a brother or sister be naked, and destitute of daily food,

"And one of you say unto them, Depart in peace, be ye warmed and filled; notwithstanding ye give them not those things which are needful to the body; what doth it profit?

"Even so faith, if it hath not works, is dead, being alone.

"Yea, a man may say, Thou hast faith, and I have works: shew me thy faith without thy works, and I will shew thee my faith by my works" (James 2:14-18).

James refers to the resultant works of those who are already saved "by grace ... through faith" (Ephesians 2:14-18). Lip-service to faith is as empty as lip-service to love.

(4) **He knew their patience:** Their faith had been tried, probably by affliction and persecution. This trial of their faith had worked patience, as James has said (James 1:2-4). Despite all the charitable deeds of service that churches or Christians may do, there will always be an unappreciative element who remain arrogant and unimpressed. If this had been the case at Thyatira, they had maintained patience through it all, and had continued doing the things their hands found to do.

(5) **He knew their works,** as He had already stated. This second mention is emphasized by the assertion that their good works had increased rather than diminished. This increase was a fruit of patience by serving even when they received little or no thanks for their kind deeds.

The Indictment

"Notwithstanding I have a few things against thee, because thou sufferest [allow] that woman Jezebel, which calleth herself a prophetess, to teach and to seduce my servants to commit fornication, and to eat things sacrificed unto idols.
"And I gave her space to repent of her fornication; and she repented not" (Revelation 2:20, 21).

The "few things" evidently included off-shoots from the principal sin. Christ was "against" them BECAUSE they allowed this horrible sin to continue, apparently unrebuked and unrestrained.

The Original Jezebel

Thyatira's indictment necessitates a brief review of the rather extended story beginning with 1 Kings 16:29 and ending with 2 Kings 9:37. It has been suggested that Ahab married Jezebel, the daughter of the king of the Zidonians, as a sort of "marriage of convenience" in view of better business relations between the two nations. At any rate, from the very start, we can see that this Zidonian Baal-worshipper was "the head of the head of the house," influencing the already evil Ahab to outrightly serve and worship her god. He built a "house of Baal" in Samaria, and "reared up an altar to Baal" in that house. Then he "made a grove" where sacrifices were offered in the open air to Baal. Through this marriage, "Ahab did more to provoke the Lord God of Israel to anger than all the kings of Israel before him" (1 Kings 16:33). The people at large followed the leadership of their king into idolatry—spiritual adultery.

When the prophet Elijah had announced a three-and-a-half-year drouth, Jezebel "cut off" and "slew the prophets of the Lord," except those whom Obadiah secretly preserved (1 Kings 18:4, 13). When the drouth ended and Elijah had the prophets of Baal slain, Jezebel was so furious that she threatened the prophet's life, which put him to flight, begging God to take his life (1 Kings 19:1-4).

About six years later, Jezebel negotiated a murder plot. (Read 1 Kings 21:1-15.) She forged the king's name and seal on letters to the elders and nobles of Israel, hypocritically

77

proclaiming a fast, and intimating that a poor man, Naboth, had blasphemed God and the king. She hired two witnesses to testify falsely against Naboth; and the order was carried out to the letter. Apparently no one knew the truth of the matter except the two accomplices whom she had bribed personally. When Jezebel told Ahab what was done, he approved, and took advantage of his covert opportunity to possess Naboth's vineyard, though Elijah prophesied his doom, and that of Jezebel.

Jezebel outlived Ahab by eleven years, but she remained the godless, vicious character she had always been. Her two sons, both kings, died tragic deaths, and in brazen defiance of King Jehu, she was thrown from an upper window and was trodden under foot and died (2 Kings 9:30-37).

Thyatira's Jezebel

History intimates that "that woman Jezebel" was a business woman, and probably involved in the guild ties mentioned earlier. It is conjectured that this marriage, too, might have been with an eye for more congenial commercial relations between the Christian and pagan elements of Thyatira.

Again from history, some manuscripts give reason to think that "Jezebel" was the pastor's wife. This line of thinking has been offered as the reason for this woman having such a preponderance of influence in the church— that she had her pastor-husband's blessing in what she was doing, and that she took advantage of this favor to usurp authority as Jezebel of old had done—to wield an ever-widening control in church matters.

If these speculations were true, she may have begun by compromising her Christian faith in order to stand in well with her guild, which was made up of a large majority of pagans. Then, as time went on, the pagan influence practically dictated her lifestyle, and soon, her doctrinal beliefs also. On the other hand, she may have been a false teacher from the start. After all, Jesus would not have called her by this infamous name if she had not been evil at heart. Who would know both Jezebels better than our timeless Lord? Though the two had lived some 1,050 years apart in time, the eternal God knew their likenesses. They were of one spirit, though their cultures were different.

This cultural difference, both in time and place, often

blinds us to the lessons we should learn from earlier periods of history. Paul tells us that Isarel's history was written for both the **admonition** and **learning** of succeeding generations (Romans 15:4; 1 Corinthians 10:11). The church at Thyatira had much to learn from the record of the earlier Jezebel. Of one thing we may be sure: Jesus was not speculating. He was right and just in emphatically saying "that woman Jezebel."

A Self-proclaimed Prophetess: Since we are considering Jesus' own words, there is no doubt that this woman's claim as a prophetess had not been a matter of church approval. Rather, she **proclaimed herself** to be a prophetess. False teachers can often be identified by their despite for church government (2 Peter 2:10; Jude 8). Since church authority does not sanction their erroneous or heretical teaching, they defy that government by proclaiming themselves "called" or "appointed" by God, boasting that "no man" has the authority to govern them in any way.

However, there is a sort of "mystical power" that accompanies this spirit, and many people stand in awe of it, afraid to withstand it, lest they be found to be fighting against God. This attitude adds strength to these false claims, leaving them to spread far and wide without hindrance.

Broadened Fields: Once they have gained an undeserved confidence, they are emboldened to teach, not just the one error they began with, but many other "new revelations"! This Jezebel, wielding the authoritative scepter of a "called prophetess," both "taught and seduced [Christ's] servants to commit fornication, and to eat things sacrificed unto idols." Though not so named, this was very much the same as the Balaamism and Nicolaitanism that was plaguing the church at Pergamos.

We must not lose sight of Christ's first and foremost indictment: "Thou sufferest that woman"—"You **allow** her to do this"—"You tolerate this heresy"—"You approve it by your silence and apathy."

Somewhere, or sometime before this letter was received at Thyatira, Jesus reveals that He had given this "Jezebel" time and opportunity to repent. Perhaps the Holy Ghost, by the mercy of God, had convicted her of her sin, but Jesus said, "she repented not." Finally the Spirit had lifted His restraint and left her to her own devices, and she mistakenly concluded that she was right after all. But not so! Note Solomon's consensus:

"Because sentence against an evil work is not executed speedily, therefore the heart of the sons of men is fully set in them to do evil.

"Though a sinner do evil an hundred times, and his days be prolonged, yet surely I know that it shall be well with them that fear God, which fear before him:

"But it shall not be well with the wicked, neither shall he prolong his days, which are as a shadow; because he feareth not before God" (Ecclesiastes 8:11-13).

ADMONITION, EXHORTATION, AND CONSEQUENCES

The Charge and the Consequences

"Behold, I will cast her into a bed, and them that commit adultery with her into great tribulation, except they repent of their deeds.

"And I will kill her children with death; and all the churches shall know that I am he which searcheth the reins and hearts: and I will give unto every one of you according to your works" (Revelation 2:22, 23).

The Charge: As always, the charge was to **repent**—both the woman and them that had yielded to her teaching and seduction. And "except they repent," Christ would punish them all, beginning with Jezebel. In fact, the original word for "I will cast" indicates that He was already in the process of executing judgment upon her. Them that had committed adultery with her would be cast into great tribulation—an unspecified form of judgmental suffering. The "space to repent" had been squandered and the time was up! Except they turn from their sin immediately, the consequences would be the bed of affliction.

As has been noted in previous lessons, the "fornication" and "adultery" were probably both spiritual and fleshly—both idolatry and lustful immorality, for low morals were a legitimate part of most idol worship. Therefore, the "bed" was a reminder of their unfaithfulness to God and their filthy lifestyle. However, the "pleasures of sin" would be gone, and only suffering for sin would remain. It is possible that diseases related to their sin would eat their life away while they were forced to face all their acquaintances with shame and remorse.

But this was not the only consequence. Jezebel's children would suffer judgment also, even unto death. They may have been among those who were deceived by her "damnable heresies" (2 Peter 2:1). And the knowledge of the destruction she had brought on her family might well have been this mother's most gnawing regret.

Now we see that God's purpose in the punishment of the Jezebelites was not limited to them. Through their judgment, He would make "all the churches" to know that His flaming eyes see all things. They would understand that He searches out and knows the deepest, darkest secrets of the heart. And they would see that, without respect of persons, He gives to every individual his due according to his works, whether good or bad (2 Corinthians 5:10). This He speaks to the whole congregation at Thyatira; the righteous as well as the evil.

The Godly Remnant Encouraged

"But unto you I say, and unto the rest in Thyatira, as many as have not this doctrine, and which have not known the depths of Satan, as they speak; I will put upon you none other burden.

"But that which ye have already hold fast till I come" (Revelation 2:24, 25).

Christ made the faithful ones aware that He knew those who had not allowed this evil woman and her cohorts to seduce them with their "depths of Satan" doctrine. It seems apparent that He was reassuring them of their Christian liberty, and that its restrictions were not burdensome or unreasonable. He may have been pointing to the decisions that had been made by the Jerusalem Council, and which had been delivered to all the churches (Acts 15:28, 29; 16:4, 5). Also, they may have recalled His words of invitation—which they had obeyed:

"Come unto me, all ye that labour and are heavy laden, and I will give you rest.

"Take my yoke upon you, and learn of me; for I am meek and lowly in heart: and ye shall find rest unto your souls.

"For my yoke is easy, and my burden is light" (Matthew 11:28-30).

No doubt Jezebel's adherents had given much lip-service to "freedom," but it was as Peter has said:

"While they [the false teachers] promise them [those they try to deceive] liberty, they themselves are the servants [slaves] of corruption: for of whom a man is overcome, of the same is he brought in bondage" (2 Peter 2:19).

Then, Paul has asked and answered a relative question:

"Know ye not, that to whom ye yield yourselves servants to obey, his servants ye are to whom ye obey; whether of sin unto death, or of obedience unto righteousness? . . .
"But now being made free from sin, and become servants to God, ye have your fruit unto holiness, and the end everlasting life.
"For the wages of sin is death; but the gift of God is eternal life through Jesus Christ our Lord" (Romans 6:16, 22, 23).

Jesus further admonished the godly remnant to faithfully hold fast this pure and holy liberty until He comes. That which they already had to their credit was their charity, service, faith, patience, and works (verse 19). Now, as Paul said to the Galatians, " . . . Let us not be weary in well-doing: for in due season we shall reap, if we faint not" (Galatians 6:9).

THE PROMISE TO THE OVERCOMER

"And he that overcometh, and keepeth my works unto the end, to him will I give power over the nations:
"And he shall rule them with a rod of iron; as the vessels of a potter shall they be broken to shivers: even as I received of my Father.
"And I will give him the morning star" (Revelation 2:26-28).

The promise here relates to the preceding charge to hold fast to, and continue, the works they were already doing; then He would give them "power over the nations." Evidently He points them ahead to the millennial reign, when the righteous who have part in the first resurrection "shall be priests of God and of Christ, and shall reign with him a thousand years" (Revelation 20:6; consider also Luke 19:15-19).

We are told that Christ shall rule "with a rod of iron" (Revelation 12:5; 19:15). The overcomer is promised a role in that reign, under Christ, of course. At that time, the inhabitants of the nations of the earth who live through "the great tribulation" will come under this rule. But their powers of rulership, as they now exist, will crumble. Christ and His Church will be the sole authority; and He will endow the overcomer with authority just as the Father has given it to Him.

Christ Himself is "the bright and morning star" (Revelation 22:16). He will give the overcomers Himself, as it were. Just as the morning star in the heavens ushers in the glorious brightness of the new day, Christ is the herald of our eternity. With Him we will have "eternal day." Hallelujah!

LISTENING TO THE LETTER

The Thyatirans Listened

As at Pergamos, some probably rejoiced while others were irritated at the contents of the letter. His introduction must have startled them. A letter from the Son of God! Could it be? Was the aged John, whose hand He used, hallucinating?

They soon discovered that He was not, for the account of their works was accurate; and certainly the words concerning "Jezebel" were true. Even she and her followers must have admitted that; but only secretly in their hearts, of course. They were probably angered at the exposure of their deception, but they could not deny that He knew them through and through.

The woman herself knew exactly when her "space to repent" had been offered. She had let it pass because the cost seemed too great—the loss of her elevated posture, her prestige as a "prophetess." To repent would have meant an open confession, the asking for forgiveness, and the proving of herself in the eyes and minds of the church, as well as those she had led astray. But now, surely they would all recognize her, even if her name was not really Jezebel. Unless her followers believed in her more than in the message of the letter, her days were numbered!

It is unrealistic to think that none of the deceived ones would have their eyes opened to the truth. What would they do? Of course, some of them might have been "sinning with their eyes open"—fully aware of what they were doing. Others might have been deluded to the awful point of "believing a lie"!

The pastor was listening, of course—listening as he read. In those flaming eyes, just where did he stand? At best, he could not help feeling the rebuke of "suffering" that woman to usurp so much authority; of allowing her, in the name of prophecy, to teach false and filthy doctrine; of allowing good people in the membership to be seduced into actual participation in this shameful affair!

How thankful the true believers must have been that they had not become involved! And how sweet must have been the Master's words of encouragement and assurance! They were strengthened in their resolve to be overcomers.

It didn't take long to read the letter—to listen to its message. But, though it may have brought about division—a sort of "pre-separation" of the sheep from the goats—in all likelihood that little church would never be the same again. The Man with feet like fine brass had walked through, as it were, and His footprints would be there a very long time.

Are WE Listening?

If God changes not (and He doesn't), and if Jesus Christ remains ever the same (and He does), then this letter to the church at Thyatira also speaks to us. After all, that was a New Testament church; a local congregation of the Church Jesus set in order and purchased with the price of His own blood. While we are nineteen hundred years nearer the culmination of the total "revelation," we are of the same dispensation of the biblical drama with the seven churches of Asia Minor. We should be listening to Christ's messages, through the Spirit, as though they had been written to us.

Are our "works" of charity, service, faith, and patience as commendable as those of the faithful ones at Thyatira? Or are we so "busy here and there" that we are actually neglecting our God-given responsibility and commission? (Read 1 Kings 20:39, 40.) Are our good works on the increase, as the need dictates? Or are we of the very large number who "get all excited" about each new opportunity to serve, and start off with great enthusiasm, only to grow tired or weary, and lose interest in just a short while?

Sometimes ministers profess a definite call of God; can hardly wait to get "on the field." Arriving there, they make a brief survey of conditions and needs. They spend hours—weeks—months—laying out their "plan of action"; they even put it into operation—a Sunday or two—maybe a month—perhaps a little longer. Then they discover that it takes work—sweat—tears—persistence—and lots of prayer. The full cooperation they expected does not come over night. The "glamour" fades; so does the "call."

Some "ambitious Jezebel" or "Balaam" with a lot of "fire" (from a lower source!) sees an opportunity to "take up the torch"—perhaps boasting a "special gift," like the "prophetess" of Thyatira. The already-tired minister is glad for somebody—anybody!—to do something—anything!—to relieve his "heavy load." So he "suffers" the "gifted" one or ones to proceed, giving minimal attention to the direction things are going. When—or if—he senses an erroneous inclination, it may already be out of hand. And that is just one way by which regrettable situations may develop.

False doctrine can be very persuasive. It has subtle beginnings, and the devil uses appealing personalities—perhaps charismatic; perhaps intellectual; perhaps super-spiritual; "gifted" in grasping "revelation"—new meanings; or whatever. Gullibility is a prevailing weakness among Christians; especially among the emotional. And gullibility's twin weakness is a blind confidence. We don't want to think that anyone is unworthy of our trust.

All of these attributes are good, providing they are genuine and God-given. Just remember—Thyatira's Jezebel CALLED HERSELF a prophetess! But "the real McCoy"—genuine through and through—is characterized by an unpretentious humility, a fervent love for the simplicity of the gospel and uncompromised, down-to-earth biblical truth.

He is not egotistic—he is sparing with "me" and "I." He is willing to serve "behind the scenes"—possibly prefers to do so; but he is subject to and cooperative with his superiors. His "call" or "ministry gift" speaks for itself—does not need to be exploited. He gives no thought to these things, but places them at God's disposal and leaves them there. He is not report-conscious, numbers-conscious, praise-conscious, or money-conscious. He simply does his best, then leaves the results to God. He covets no personal acclaim. God alone is to be glorified.

The four churches we have studied thus far have all been plagued by some form of heresy or false doctrine, **operating within**! In His earthly ministry, Jesus often warned the disciples about false teachers. In His "Sermon on the Mount" He began with the Pharisees' erroneous interpretations of Scripture and closed with a fearful warning against false prophets and their impressive claims. Over and over He alerts us about deceit. (Read Matthew 5:21-48; 6:1-18; 15:9; 16:6-12; 24:4-13, 24-26; Mark 7:7; 13:5, 6, 21-23; Luke 21:1.) Some sixty years after His ascension, He found the Asian churches infested with this problem.

It will be well to consider that deceivers are able to gain their greatest following by "counterfeit," so to speak. Counterfeits are so near in appearance to that which they are imitating that even the most watchful may be duped. Jesus declared (and, of course He knows!) that through "great signs and wonders . . . if it were possible, they shall deceive the very elect" (Matthew 24:24).

Are we as watchful as we should be? Do we have the discernment necessary to detect the Balaamism, Nicolaitanism, and Jezebelism in the highly "spiritual" show of the supposed "miraculous"? How impressed are we by the "great swelling words" of flattering "admiration [for] advantage" (Jude 16) flooding the ether waves today? Do we recognize Jezebel's "prophecies" for the deadly deception they convey? Do imposing, vibrant personalities make us gullible—"easily cheated or tricked" (Webster)?

Do we show respect of persons by tolerating wrongdoing because "She's the pastor's wife," or "the overseer's daughter"? Or, "He's from a long-time important family in the Church"? Or, "He's a faithful tithe-payer and a generous giver"?

Do we entertain a lenient tolerance toward fornication, adultery and adulterous marriages, and "other religions," which the Bible has already labeled for the fiery pit?

We must re-emphasize the fact that the thing Jesus held

against this pastor and/or local church (in business conference, we would say) was their ALLOWING this woman to continue in whatever capacity of leadership she held. If she was under appointment, she should not have been. If she was usurping authority, or teaching "behind the doors" from house to house, both she and those who stood with her should have been disciplined, and excluded if necessary, by the church. Jesus was against the pastor and church at Thyatira for allowing this evil leaven to spread through the membership; and He is against us today if we do likewise.

It is time to LISTEN—with our EYES open as well as our EARS! Jesus said, "WATCH and PRAY . . . "!

—Lesson Seven—

THE CHURCH AT SARDIS

RELATION OF CITY AND CHURCH

Geographical, Cultural, and Historical Situation

Geography: Sardis, in the district of Lydia, was thirty-five miles southeast of Thyatira and fifty miles east of Smyrna. It was built on the slopes of the Mount Tmolus range, between the Hermus and Pactolus Rivers. It was at the intersection of five roads—trade routes from the interior to the Aegean Sea.

Sardis was one of the world's wealthiest trade centers, the source of that wealth being its commerce, its textiles, wool dyes, jewelry, and the products of the valley's rich soil. But its power and wealth eventually worked its ruin.

Culture and History: One writer, without elaboration, dates the founding of Sardis as 1200 B.C. In about 556 B.C., Croesus, king of Lydia, ushered in "the Golden Age of Sardis" from the wealth gathered from the gold mines and trade. But King Cyrus of Persia took the city in 546 B.C., and he is said to have taken $600,000,000 worth of treasure. In 344 B.C. Sardis surrendered to Alexander the Great, but was taken by Antiochus the Great in 214 B.C. He in turn was defeated by the Romans in 190 B.C., and it was under Roman rule when the church received the letter on record in Revelation 3:1-6.

Mystery cults from the ancient East abounded in Sardis. The principal temple was the Temple of Cybele (Artemis), which was both massive and magnificent. **Andrew Tait** in his "Messages to the Seven Churches of Asia," says of "the mother goddess, Cybele": "Her worship was of the most debasing character, and orgies like those of Dionysus were practiced at the festivals held in her honor. Sins of the foulest and darkest impurity were committed on those occasions...."

Despite these cults, Sardis early became a center of Christianity in Asia Minor. But **Matthew Henry** rather sums it up as follows: "[Sardis was] the first city in that part of the world that was converted by the preaching of John; and, some say, the first that revolted from Christianity; and one of the first that was laid to ruins, in which it still lies, without any church or ministry.

What was ancient Sardis is now a desolate region with scarcely an inhabitant. A nearby village is called Sart.

CHRIST INTRODUCES HIMSELF

"And unto the angel of the church in Sardis write; These things saith he that hath the seven Spirits of God, and the seven stars . . . " (Revelation 3:1).

As we read the entire letter, we will see that Christ's introduction called their attention to Himself as having all they needed for the recovery they must make if they were to survive.

(1) **He has the seven Spirits of God.** The church at Sardis was a dying church. In all probability Christ intended His words for the pastor, then for the church. We are reminded of a period in Israel's history when something much greater than the power and ability of men was required for their need.

The remnant of the exiled children of God were returning to their homeland. The temple was in disrepair and there had been much hindrance. The foundations had been laid, then the work had been stopped. Zerubbabel had been appointed governor of returning Israel by Cyrus, king of Persia, and had undertaken this work of restoration. After a lapse of several years, the prophets Haggai and Zechariah prophesied that the work should be taken up again (Ezra 5:1, 2; Haggai 1:1 through 2:4). Zechariah was a visionary prophet, and in his seventh of ten visions, an angel gave some specific directions:

" . . . This is the word of the Lord unto Zerubbabel, saying, Not by might, nor by power, but by my spirit, saith the Lord of hosts.

"Who art thou, O great mountain [of opposition]? before Zerubbabel thou shalt become a plain: and he shall bring forth the headstone thereof with shoutings, crying, Grace, grace unto it.

"Moreover the word of the Lord came unto me, saying,

"The hands of Zerubbabel have laid the foundation of this house; his hands shall also finish it; and thou shalt know that the Lord of hosts hath sent me unto you" (Zechariah 4:6-9).

God encouraged Zerubbabel through the promise of His grace, and power, and might by His Spirit; not by man's might, as by a great army, nor by authority from earthly sources. And, in obedience to the Spirit of the Lord, Zerubbabel directed the completion of the temple (Ezra 6:15, 16).

At Sardis, the church was at a standstill. Something had caused them to falter, and Jesus was telling them that the solution was by the Spirit of God. Undoubtedly He was expecting the "star," or pastor, to rise up as Zerubbabel had done, and follow the instructions He was about to give. The "seven Spirits of God" are mentioned also in Revelation 1:4 and 5:6. Since we know from the Word of truth rightly divided that there is but one Spirit (Ephesians 4:4), it seems clear that Christ's reference to "seven Spirits of God" has to do with the plurality of manifestations, diversities, administrations, and operations of the Holy Ghost (1 Corinthians 12:4-7). If we would insist on "seven" (the biblical number for perfection, or completion), Isaiah 11:1-5 has been cited by many expositors, where a sevenfold characterization is noted as resting on Christ: (a) The Spirit of the Lord; (b) the spirit of wisdom; (c) the spirit of understanding; (d) the spirit of counsel; (e) the spirit of might; (f) the spirit of knowledge; and (g) the spirit of the fear of the Lord.

The one and only Christ is "made unto us" many things—"wisdom, and righteousness, and sanctification, and redemption" (1 Corinthians 1:30). He is the Son of man, the Son of God. "God with us," Saviour, Lord, the Word made flesh, the Way, the Truth, the Life, the true Vine, the Bread of life, the good shepherd, the door of the sheep, and much more; yet but one Christ. Likewise, the Holy Ghost is one, but with many attributes through which He ministers not only to the Church as a body, but also to every individual believer.

Christ is the one Mediator between God and man (1 Timothy 2:5). Since the day of Pentecost, He has mediated through the Holy Ghost. He has gone away, but He prayed the Father to give us "another Comforter." In this way, Christ is still with us—"I will come to you" (John 14:16-18). Technically, the Father gave Him the Holy Ghost to send to us (John 15:26; 16:7). Now, notice carefully how the Spirit dispenses "all truth"—"all things":

"I have yet many things to say unto you, but ye cannot bear them now.

"Howbeit when he, the Spirit of truth, is come, he will guide you into all truth: for he shall not speak of himself; but whatsoever he shall hear, that shall he speak: and he will shew you things to come.

"He shall glorify me: for he shall receive of mine, and shall shew it unto you.

"All things that the Father hath are mine: therefore said I, that he shall take of mine, and shall shew it unto you" (John 16:12-15).

A "mediator" is one who brings about intervention, or reconciliation; a "middle man" who considers both parties and strives to bring about peace and accord. Jesus is that Mediator in our context, the greatest example of His mediatorship being reconciliation between God, the offended, the man, the offender (2 Corinthians 5:18, 19). But according to the verses cited above in John 16, "all things" are mediated between God and His "sons" through the instrumentality of the Holy Ghost. The entire Trinity is involved. "All things that the Father hath" are also Christ's. The Holy Ghost takes the things of Christ and shows them to us—apparently by the operation of "the seven Spirits of God," as it were.

Another interesting thought in this connection was presented by John the Baptist when he contrasted the measure of the Spirit that was upon himself with the measure that was on Christ:

"For he whom God hath sent [Christ] speaketh the words of God: for God giveth not the Spirit by measure unto him.

"The Father loveth the Son, and hath given ALL THINGS into his hand" (John 3:34, 35).

(2) **He has the seven stars**. Pastors—and all ministers—are accountable to Christ. They are responsible as His representatives. This should make them faithful to their "holy calling" (2 Timothy 1:9)—their "heavenly calling" (Hebrews 3:1-6). He is their example in faithfulness, and they should "consider" this well!

Since both "the seven Spirits of God" and "the seven stars" are in His possession, it is thus indicated that the Holy Ghost works through the ministry, and He has all the spiritual influences they need for their work.

The condition of the church at Sardis declared their need for the fulness of the Spirit; and the pastor was reminded of his **responsibility** and **accountability** as having been placed at Sardis by Christ, or by the will of God.

CHRIST'S APPRAISAL OF THE CHURCH

"I know thy works, that thou hast a name that thou livest, and art dead.

"... For I have not found thy works perfect before God.

"Thou hast a few names even in Sardis which have not defiled their garments; and they shall walk with me in white: for they are worthy" (Revelation 3:1, 2, 4).

The Indictments

Christ began His appraisal with a sharp rebuke, rather than with commendation. **John F. Walvoord**, in "The Revelation of Jesus Christ," prefaces their condition in plain language, as follows:

> The church at Sardis evidently had a reputation among the churches in the area, and was considered a spiritual church, and one that had an effective ministry and testimony for God. From the divine viewpoint, however, it is considered a church that had only a name of being alive, and actually was dead as far as spiritual life and power were concerned. This searching judgment of Christ as it relates to the church of Sardis is one to be pondered by the modern church, which often is full of activity even though there is little that speaks of Christ and spiritual life and power.

William Barclay, in "Letters to the Seven Churches," says that a church is "in danger of death when it begins to worship its own past... When it is more concerned with forms than with life... When it loves systems more than it loves Jesus Christ... When it is more concerned with material than spiritual things."

Inward Realities: Somehow the church at Sardis had "made a name for itself." If that "lively name" had been justified, it would mean that there was a time when it had had Christ's approval without consciously seeking outside commendation.

Most, at least, of the members had had genuine experiences with God, the attainment of which had necessitated humility and a close walk with the Lord. Service—both in good works and in worship—had been spontaneous; the natural result of a spiritual life and the fulness of God's life.

It had been alive with the activity of evangelical outreach and practical works correspondent with true faith. It had been a praying church, carrying every problem to God for solution, and every perplexity for His clarification. His Word had been a lamp at hand to guide their feet, and a beacon to light the more distant course of life. They had depended on that light and had given heed to its every direction and its every restraint. They had enjoyed "the unity of the Spirit in the bond of peace" (Ephesians 4:3)—the peace OF God and Peace WITH God and one another.

It is probable that many individuals had been inspired by the members at Sardis, and that other churches had righteously coveted the spirit of this local congregation.

We repeat—this glowing picture was probable providing the "living name" had once been justified.

Outward Appearances: How fluently we tend to quote God's words to Samuel—". . . The Lord seeth not as man seeth; for man looketh on the outward appearance, but the Lord looketh on the heart" (1 Samuel 16:7)! Usually it is intended to confirm that our hearts are approved of God even though our fellowmen may judge us otherwise on the basis of outward conduct or appearance. At times, this is the case; however, in the original context, the outward appearance appealed to even the godly Samuel, but not to God. And so it was with the church at Sardis. Its "name" belied its true character.

Jesus did not elaborate on the deathly nature of their "works," neither their causes. He knew that they would arrive at His meaning if they would only accept His word that they were "dead" and bring themselves under an unbiased self-examination. While we are not to presume to judge the specifics of their dead or dying condition, we may certainly be admonished by a number of possibilities as we consider our own current situation.

(1) **Empty professions of faith**. Sometimes one generation of believers fails to articulate the true basis of faith in Christ to the succeeding generation. Too much is left to assumption; it is only assumed that real experiential salvation, sanctification, and Spirit baptism are understood, and are being earnestly sought and truly obtained. Without a genuine heart-relationship with God, past realities become mere mimicry— pretentious and lifeless.

The succeeding generations may be less to blame than the generation which neglected to convey the truth to their posterity. It is easy—and comforting—to boast. "My children all cut their teeth on Church of God benches," but the question is: Are they SAVED? Are they WHOLLY SANCTIFIED? Are they FILLED WITH THE HOLY GHOST?

Even affirmative answers to these questions are meaningless unless the experiences are grounded on the Word of God and bear biblical evidence. It is important that we insist on these basics, for, if these experiences are not genuine, the empty professions are deadly deceptive. Souls which are precious to us and to God may be eternally lost while they are led to think they are right with God.

This state of affairs is usually the result of the Word of God not being preached and taught; yea, expounded, or explained in detail, making sure it is thoroughly understood. Casual mention of "a vital relationship with God" is meaningless and can be misleading if it is only assumed that the hearers know what such a relationship is, and how it is attained.

Salvation, sanctification, and the indwelling Holy Ghost give life to the individual, and maintain that life. Without the members being spiritually alive, the church will be dead.

Take a church, for example, with every member scripturally alive. With the passing of time, some will move away; some will die. Every one may be replaced by "recruitment," as it were, so that the membership is maintained, or even increased, numerically. But if those replacements have only empty professions, that church will be a gradually dying church; and by and by it will be spiritually dead.

(2) **A dying love**. We have already studied the church at Ephesus, whose indictment by the Lord was, "Thou hast left

thy first love." That church still had many things to commend it, but without their "first love," its life would diminish until its candlestick would be removed. Like the Ephesian saints, those at Sardis apparently were very active, since they had not as yet lost their name as being alive. But without love for God, and a correspondent love for one another as children of God, activity is only vanity. It counts for nothing with the Lord.

A church may appear to be retaining a life from past "glories"; a past when love was there and motivated every good work. Its "history" may be repeated annually in commemoration, but only mechanically. Instead of "glory," it becomes "vainglory." Even the "historical worship" may be retained, but in form only. Memory may be so vivid that there is even a showing of spiritual demonstrations. They were so much a part of the worship of "the system" that they are still treasured by way of a "traditional fire." The sad thing is that this "form" may come to be thought of as the "power." In the eyes of others, the church may continue to have "a name that thou livest," but in the all-knowing mind and all-seeing eye of God, it is "dead."

(3) **"At ease in Zion."** No mention is made in the Sardis letter of church problems—heresies, immorality, false claims of apostleship or special gifts, blasphemous boastings, tribulations, martyrdom, poverty—such as were found at Ephesus, Smyrna, Pergamos, and Thyatira. The only problem cited was a "creeping death," of which they seemingly were not aware.

The prophet Amos has left us the record of a similar period in Israel's history, beginning with "Woe to them that are at ease in Zion" (Amos 6:1; read through verse 8). It seems that there were two interlinked causes for the judgments of verses 7 and 8: (a) **An unappreciated prosperity**, and (b) **wealth**. Their wealth was the result of their prosperity. While both may come from the hand of God, both have proven to be the Christian's greatest test; certainly the most dangerous to spirituality. Their danger lies in the fact that they are often, if not usually, misunderstood and misused, or abused.

God prospers His people because He loves them, and He trusts them for an acceptable response. David said, "Let the Lord be magnified, which hath pleasure in the prosperity of his servant" (Psalms 35:27). The godly young Joseph prospered even in adversity (Genesis 39:3, 23). When God is pleased to prosper His servants, they should find pleasure in serving Him.

Paul made a statement which, though somewhat out of context here, is nonetheless true: "... She that liveth in pleasure [for pleasure's sake] is dead while she liveth" (1 Timothy 5:6). In Amos' day, Israel misused God's prosperity for pleasure—its comforts, its luxuries, its idleness, its revelry, and eventually its debauchery. They cast to the wind their responsibility and concern for the "affliction of Joseph," and selfishly "lived it up." And God was displeased. He abhorred their carefree attitude—their gluttony, their banqueting, their putting "far away the evil day."

Now at Sardis, Christ reveals His appraisal of a similar situation in His Church. She is "dead," though she glories in having a "name" as being alive—"dead while she liveth"!

Wealth tends to gender covetousness—a greed for more and more. Paul may surprise us with his intimation that material gain can be mistakenly considered as "godliness," which shows us just how deceitful unconsecrated wealth can be:

"... Supposing that gain is godliness ....

"But godliness with contentment is great gain.

"For we brought nothing into this world, and it is certain that we can carry nothing out.

"And having food and raiment let us be therewith content.

"But they that will be rich fall into temptation and a snare, and into many foolish and hurtful lusts, which drown men in destruction and perdition.

"For the love of money is the root of all evil: which while some coveted after, they have erred from the faith, and pierced themselves through with many sorrows ....

"Charge them that are rich in this world, that they be not highminded, nor trust in uncertain riches, but in the living God, who giveth us richly all things to enjoy;

"That they do good, that they be rich in good works, ready to distribute, willing to communicate;

"Laying up in store for themselves a good foundation against the time to come, that they may lay hold on eternal life" (1 Timothy 6:5-10, 17-19).

If the church at Sardis was being tried, it was by prosperity; and they were failing the test—as so many are doing today!

(4) **Internal pride.** Having gained the "name," this church may have been taking pride in being "in the limelight." Perhaps other churches scanned the various "Top Ten" columns to see if Sardis had made it again.

A little "friendly competition" may be commendable within limits; but the old adage, "Figures don't lie," will bear some qualification. A "working church" is not always a "living church," or a "victorious church." One church's five thousand dollars and "an increase in everything" may be less praiseworthy before God than another church's hundred dollars along with a decrease here and there. God would have everyone to do his best; and He is the best judge of the "results."

Remember what Jesus said about the broad-phylacteried, chief-seated, breast-beating, long-praying, proselyting, hypocritical Pharisees (Matthew 23; Luke 18:9-14)? "Verily I say unto you, THEY HAVE THEIR REWARD" (Matthew 6:2, 5, 16). In other words, they desired to be seen and heard; they sought the praise and glory of men; they wanted to be noted for their outward appearances. They received all of those things from a gullible public, and that was their reward—THEIR ONLY REWARD! They may have died with "a good report" on the church's records, being lauded loud and long at their funeral. But they were not only dead, but "twice dead"!

(5) **Compromised truth.** Living in the midst of a grossly secular society, where immorality knows no restraint and integrity is only a word, temptation to compromise God's Word of truth is strong. Sound doctrine, such as holiness of life, the sacredness of and faithfulness to the marriage vows, honoring covenant relationships, abstinence from liquor, drugs and tobacco, and separation from the things of the world, is often disregarded or given less restricted meaning.

Early pangs of conscience are soon quieted, and self-justification pleads "wisdom," "freedom," and "no harm." Spiritual death comes slowly. Like the frog that was put in cool water which was heated gradually to the boiling point, bringing its death without the least resistance—numbly and without suffering—even so one compromise after another soon results in SIN, but under "pretty names." "And the wages of sin is DEATH" (Romans 6:23), alike to the unbeliever and the backslidden Christian or church member.

Imperfect works

"Air-beating" activity seldom bears profitable fruit. It is like the seeds that fall among thorns and "Bring no fruit to perfection" (Luke 8:14). Jesus knew their works—knew they were "busy"—but He reprimanded them for their imperfect, incomplete accomplishments. It was as though the "busyness" had been their main goal; anything to keep up the cherished "name"!

ADMONITION, EXHORTATION, AND CONSEQUENCES

The Charge

"Be watchful, and strengthen the things which remain, that are ready to die . . .

"Remember therefore how thou hast received and heard, and hold fast, and repent" (Revelation 3:2, 3).

Jesus gave them four specific admonishments:

(1) **Be watchful.** It may be that Jesus used the history of the city to remind the church to be watchful. Sardis, twice at least, had fallen before invaders, even though the city was ideally situated high above the valley so that surprise attacks need not have occurred. Their overthrow came about through their overconfidence and failure to be on the alert. At the time of this letter, the attack was spiritual and the invader was Satan. The church seemed insensitive to his inner workings in the midst; his subtle, quiet take-over! One writer has said, "The real danger of our age is that we may lose preception of the real goal and end of all our labor in the multiplied machinery that carries it on."

No business venture can safely go on month after month and year after year without periodic inventories. If the "machinery" is not functioning properly, the problem is discovered early and adjustments and corrections are made before great losses accumulate. Why should we think that the Church need not undergo careful scrutiny by those responsible for its spiritual progress?

(2) **Strengthen the remains.** As verse 4 reveals, a few

individuals were remaining true, though the church itself was "dead." Although the "escape" would be exceedingly narrow, there might be a "resurrection" by strengthening the little that was left, but it must be done without delay since Jesus saw the remains as "ready to die," or barely alive. They were so closely associated with the overwhelming influences of death that they would soon succumb!

(3) **Remember ... hold fast**. They had once received the truth upon hearing it. Jesus admonished them to remember how it came about in the beginning of their faith, then to take a new grasp of it and hold it fast. Perhaps by listening to the few who remained, a fresh breath of gospel truth would revive their spirits, saving them from total ruin. Then, realizing how near they had come to utter extinction, they would take a firmer grasp, never again to become encoiled in a "living death"!

(4) **Repent**. The tense of the verbs "hold fast" and "repent" in the original text indicates that they were to continue to hold fast the truth, and to make this a **once-for-all** repentance. According to James, a wavering, vacillating faith is too unstable to receive anything from the Lord (James 1:6-8).

Take notice that mere reformation and new resolve is not sufficient. As always, genuine repentance and turning away from the path of failure is mandatory. Good works do not cease, but their motivation is adjusted. "Name" or no name, it is God who is to be glorified in all that we do.

It takes true humility to confess failure and repent with godly sorrow. The Apostle Peter says:

"Humble yourselves therefore under the mighty hand of God, that he may exalt you in due time:

"Casting all your care upon him; for he careth for you.

"Be sober, be vigilant; because your adversary the devil, as a roaring lion, walketh about, seeking whom he may devour:

"Whom resist stedfast in the faith, knowing that the same afflictions are accomplished in your brethren that are in the world" (1 Peter 5:6-8).

The Consequences

"If therefore thou shalt not watch, I will come on thee

as a thief, and thou shalt not know what hour I will come upon thee.

"Thou hast a few names even in Sardis which have not defiled their garments; and they shall walk with me in white: for they are worthy" (Revelation 3:3, 4).

Apparently, Satan had come among them "as a thief," unsuspected, unrecognized, because they had not been watchful. He had gained an advantage, even though they should not have been "ignorant of his devices" (2 Corinthians 2:11).

Now, Jesus stated the inevitable consequence if they should refuse to heed His command to watch. He would "come on" or "upon" them "as a thief," unexpectedly or suddenly, bringing judgment upon them!

A thief takes those things which are most valuable. Christ—not a thief, but "*as* a thief"—will remove the "remaining enjoyments and mercies, not by fraud [as a thief would do], but in justice and righteousness" (Matthew Henry), if we forfeit things of eternal worth for things that are temporal (2 Corinthians 4:18).

The righteous not forsaken: The Church is a God-ordained entity, precious in His sight. However, too many have been the instances when it has temporarily lost sight of its fundamental purpose. David asks a question which may be relevant in more than one context: "If the foundations be destroyed, what can the righteous do?" (Psalms 11:3).

In their frustration over the dead-but-active local church, the "few" whom the Lord counts "worthy" may feel a dreadful sense of "let-down." But the church does not save. Only Christ can save; and here we have His reassurance that He knows each individual. As Paul had said, "Nevertheless the foundation of God standeth sure, having this seal, The Lord knoweth them that are his" (2 Timothy 2:19). He knows them individually.

"Defiled garments" may have reference to the individual's love for and participation in the things of the world. Even more relevant are the works of self-righteousness, which are "as filthy rags" when contrasted with the purity and holiness of God (Isaiah 64:6; Titus 3:5; Ephesians 2:8, 9). Except for the efficacy of Christ's work in our behalf in being made sin for us (2 Corinthians 5:21), we would be cast off as an unclean thing. But by belief in His perfect work for us, our "faith is COUNTED for righteousness" (Romans 4:5). In the strictest sense, no man is "worthy" except as God sees us in His Son, who paid and cancelled our sin debt.

There were some in the church at Sardis thus counted worthy, having been cleansed by the blood of the Lamb in justification and sanctification, then keeping their garments clean and white by remaining in "the cleansing stream." These, even through eternity, will walk with Christ as being worthy.

THE PROMISE TO THE OVERCOMER

"He that overcometh, the same shall be clothed in white raiment; and I will not blot out his name out of the book of life, but I will confess his name before my Father, and before his angels" (Revelation 3:5).

The promise in verse 4 applies to "he that overcometh," including the "white raiment," which is "the righteousness of saints" (Revelation 19:8). Those with nothing but a "name," carried over from a past when they apparently had been counted worthy of it, should have been alarmed at the thought of their names being removed from "the book of life"! God grant that they repented; but we do not know that they did. However, the "worthy' ones were assured that their names would remain, and would be there to testify for them at the judgment. (See Revelation 13:8; 17:8; 20:12, 15; 21:27; and 22:19.)

Then there was the promise that He would confess their name before the Father and His angels. He had said this before, while He walked among men:

"Whosoever therefore shall confess me before men, him will I confess also before my Father which is in heaven.

"But whosoever shall deny me before men, him will I also deny before my Father which is in heaven" (Matthew 10:32,33).

"Also I say unto you, Whosoever shall confess me before men, him shall the Son of man also confess before the angels of God:

"But he that denieth me before men shall be denied before the angels of God" (Luke 12:8, 9).

LISTENING TO THE LETTER

Sardis Listened

Being a church with a "name" of commendation, as others saw them, the members at Sardis may have gathered in expectation of high praise from Christ also. Even the "worthy" ones, not being judgmental of their brethren, may have thought that all was well.

Remember Jesus' preview of the coming day when there will be a division of the "sheep" from the "goats"? The "sheep," who will have served with no thought of praise or special reward, will be surprised to hear the Lord's enumeration of their commendable works. But the "goats" will be just as surprised to hear Him say, "Depart from me," either because they have done nothing, or because they have done it for vainglory, in self-righteousness (Matthew 25:31-46).

Upon hearing the Master's indictment, "Thou hast a name that thou livest, and art dead," what was their reaction? Were they shocked—stunned by the surprise rebuff—jolted to reality? Were they "hurt" or offended—claiming that He had not appreciated them for their "much working"? Were they angry because He openly discounted their "name" and laid bare the truth before the eyes of all who had thought of them as an example? Were they jealous of the "few" who were called "worthy" to walk with Him in white garments?

And those who were commended—did they shed tears of humble gratitude? Or were they sorely tempted to glory against their reproved brethren? Perhaps they remembered Paul's words:

> "But he that glorieth, let him glory in the Lord.
> "For not he that commendeth himself is approved, but whom the Lord commendeth" (2 Corinthians 10:17, 18).

This we know: They all heard the truth about themselves as God saw them and knew them to be. If they presumed to argue with God, they showed themselves foolish, as was true with Job. After the Great Sovereign had held His peace in the face of Job's contentions, God challenged him to answer one question:

"Shall he that contendeth [disputes, argues, debates] with the Almighty instruct him? he that reproveth God, let him answer it [the question]" (Job 40:2).

If indeed the church at Sardis was tempted to such contention, we trust that their answer agreed with Job's:

"Behold, I am vile; what shall I answer thee? I will lay mine hand upon my mouth.
"Once have I spoken; but I will not answer: yea, twice; but I will proceed no further" (Job 40:4, 5).

Are WE Listening?
In the thinking of many people, LIFE means LIVELINESS. To them, ENERGY means MOTION, and POWER means SPECTACULAR ACTIVITY. A little quiet meditation or unadorned COMMON SENSE will bring us to the conclusion that such thinking may SOMETIMES be true, but OFTENTIMES false.

A humorous quip from "years gone by" comes to mind by way of illustration: The owner of a "tin lizzy" automobile bragged that it would make seventy-five miles per hour. After the guffawing of his listeners quieted down, he explained—"It goes twenty-five miles an hour straight ahead and fifty up and down."

Actually, it requires very little life, energy, or power to produce a lot of movement or a thunderous noise. The old coal-fired locomotives used to whistle loud and long at every crossing—**on the level plains!** But when they approached **the incline** to "the high country," the whistling was reduced to a minimum. All the steam in the boiler was needed to pull the tremendous load on the upgrade.

Likewise, the quiet "white heat" in the forge is the fire that "gets into the iron," even though the roaring, billowing "first flash" may cause much more excitement.

Let's face it: A church seldom has a "name" as being "alive" unless its "spiritual demonstration" is great. It may be making little or no progress forward. The "direction" it is traveling is camouflaged by the volume of its worship and the "business" of its "program schedule." Its "fire" must be SEEN, even if the "iron" is not affected. Its "whistle" must be HEARD in order to maintain the "name that thou livest."

After all, that laborious "chug-chug" up the mountainside has far less "appeal."

Are we listening to Jesus' message to us, passed on from Sardis? Is our church alive in name only? Are our garments merely **soiled** from laboring with Him in sin's gutter, or are they **defiled** with the filth of our own egotistical, self-righteous, vainglorious hurry-scurry? Are we in line for the eventual change to "white raiment"?

Are we, as individual believers and members of the Body, confessing His name by the example of the overcomer's uprightness—all for His glory?

A good name is something to be cherished, providing it is deserved. Solomon—who might better have followed his own proverb—said: "A good name is rather to be chosen than great riches . . . " (Proverbs 22:1). And the "works" that merit that name are essential as long as they glorify God—as Jesus said:

> "Let your light so shine before men, that they may see your good works, and glorify your Father which is in heaven" (Matthew 5:16).

"LET" it shine; not MAKE it shine. If the light of God's love is in us, it will shine if it is allowed to shine—and providing the vessel (globe) is kept unsmudged—unreproachful.

As living saints, let us never forget that, like Paul, the LIFE that we live as Christians is "by the faith of the Son of God, who loved me, and gave himself for me" (Galatians 2:20). Paradoxically, we are "dead," yet we "live by faith." Again Paul says:

> "For ye [the old man] are dead, and your life [the new man] is hid with Christ in God.
>
> "When Christ, WHO IS OUR LIFE, shall appear, then shall ye also appear with him in glory" (Colossians 3:3, 4).

" . . . In white raiment." Hallelujah!

—Lesson Eight—
THE CHURCH AT PHILADELPHIA
RELATION OF CITY AND CHURCH
The Geographical, Cultural, and Historical Situation

Geography: Philadelphia was located on the border between the districts of Lydia and Mysia, about thirty miles southeast of Sardis on the road to Laodicea. It was on the Cogamus River (a branch of the Hermus) at the base of the Mount Tmolus range, which was an ancient volcano. The city was situated on a broad, low hill—a position making it easy to defend when other powers tried to take it.

The **Thompson Bible Survey** says: "The city was an outpost of Greek culture, a show place for Hellenism, on the Roman Post Road, the commercial artery between Rome and the East." Beautiful temples and public buildings graced the boulevards.

The surrounding area is still rich agriculturally. Grapes are one of the principal crops. Though earthquakes have been frequent and sometimes greatly destructive, the rich soil and favorable location have caused it to remain well populated.

Culture and History: Philadelphia is said to have been founded about 159-138 B.C. by Attalus Philadelphus, King of Pergamum. As a result of the Roman Conquest in the second century B.C., Philadelphia, as a part of Asia Minor, came under Roman rule, and it remained so at the time John sent the letter to the church.

Philadelphia was a center for the worship of Dionysus, the Greek god of vegetation and wine. Little else is said about "religion" until the Christian era.

It is not known how the church came to be established there. Conjectures offered have included: (1) Some Christian influence filtering into a Jewish synagogue and developing into a church; or (2) some who were at the Feast of Pentecost when the Holy Ghost descended may have returned home converted, leading to the development of the church; or (3) possibly some of Paul's associates evangelized the area. However, as in many other places, the Jews were the Christians' fiercest opponents; but this church, though possibly small, was stedfast.

At this present time, there are still some active Christians in Philadelphia, but the number is not known. The modern Turkish name is Alasehir.

CHRIST INTRODUCES HIMSELF

"And to the angel of the church in Philadelphia write; These things saith he that is holy, he that is true, he that hath the key of David, he that openeth, and no man shutteth; and shutteth, and no man openeth" (Revelation 3:7).

The church in Philadelphia is one of the seven with the distinction of having no indictment against it by Christ. It is fitting, therefore, that He should introduce Himself in the above manner.

"He that is holy"
All the persons in the Trinity are equally holy. God is referred to over and over in the Scriptures as being holy: "... The Lord our God is holy" (Psalms 99:9), for example. (See also Joshua 24:19; 1 Samuel 6:20; Isaiah 5:15; John 7:28; 17:11; Revelation 4:8).

Christ is the Holy One: "ye denied the Holy One and the Just" (Acts 3:14). Even the devils acknowledged this: "I know who thou art; the Holy One of God" (Luke 4:34; see also Acts 4:27, 30; Revelation 6:10; 15:4).

The third person of the Godhead is the Holy Ghost (Mark 1:8; Acts 2:4; John 14:26; Acts 11:15); or the Holy Spirit (Luke 11:13; Ephesians 1:13; 4:30; 1 Thessalonians 4:8).

Christ is preeminently holy, having been conceived by the Holy Ghost (Matthew 1:18, 20; Luke 1:35), and was not the seed of the fallen Adam. Thus He identifies Himself with the very holiness of God and the Holy Ghost. Proclaiming Him as the true High Priest, the author of the **Epistle to the Hebrews** speaks of His qualification as being "holy, harmless, undefiled, separate from sinners, and made higher than the heavens" (Hebrews 7:26).

As our Holy High Priest, He was also sinless—"... in all points tempted like as we are, yet without sin" (Hebrews 4:15). Perhaps the saints at Philadelphia remembered this verse of Scripture and could associate His temptation without sinning to their own trial of faith in the face of Jewish contentions (verses 8, 9). They may have read Peter's encouragement unto holy living:

> "Wherefore gird up the loins of your mind, be sober, and hope to the end for the grace that is to be brought unto you at the revelation of Jesus Christ;
> "As obedient children, not fashioning yourselves according to the former lusts in your ignorance:
> "But as he which hath called you is holy, so be ye holy in all manner of conversation [behavior]" (1 Peter 1:13-16).

Their stedfastness could have been rooted in such admonition as: "Follow peace with all men, and [follow] holiness, without which no man shall see the Lord" (Hebrew 12:14). Now, what an affirmation it was to receive this letter from Him who is holy!

"He that is true"

Christ is the very embodiment of "true holiness," or holiness according to **truth**. One example is found in the context of Ephesians 4:17-24.

The truth concerning the separated life is "in Jesus" (verse 21); and the "new man" that we are by virtue of His redemption is "created in [God's] righteousness and **true** holiness" (verse 24).

"He that is true" had declared earlier to His disciples. "I AM the ... TRUTH" (John 14:6). He is "the TRUE Light" (John 1:9); "the TRUE bread from heaven" (John 6:32); "the TRUE vine" (John 15:1). He is "the Word" (John 1:1, 2, 14), and the Word is TRUTH (John 17:17).

Not only is He "true" in the sense of truth itself, but He is true in the sense of faithfulness and fidelity; He is constant—unwavering—dependable. This had great meaning to a church that had stood true to Him when they might have suffered less, temporarily, by making compromises with the Jewish false claims.

The two aspects—"holy" and "true"—complement each other, for **right doctrine** and **right living** belong together. There can be no holiness without truth. Christ cannot lie; He is the very fountain of truth. Lastly, as children of God by faith in His work on Calvary, we also must be "true":

"And we know that the Son of God is come, and hath given us an understanding, that we may know HIM THAT IS TRUE, and we are in HIM THAT IS TRUE, even in his Son Jesus Christ. This is the true God, and eternal life" (1 John 5:20).

"He that hath the key of David"

This must be understood in the light of what follows, especially in verse 9, where the Jews were making false claims. They had forfeited their right to the ongoing fulfillment of God's plan of the ages when they rejected their Messiah.

From the time of Christ's advent and sacrifice as the promised Saviour of the world—not only of "His people," the Jews (Matthew 1:21), but of "all people" (Luke 2:10), the true Jew has been, and is, "whosoever believeth in him" and His Gospel, accepting Him as Messiah, Saviour, and Lord of all.

The "key of David," or "the house of David," was passed on from generation to generation, as is seen in the prophecy of Isaiah to which Jesus evidently referred in His letter to the Philadelphians (Isaiah 22:22). God never forgot His covenant with David, which always pointed to its fulfillment in Christ. In the expectation of God, the house of David was to accept the new covenant of grace as a continuation of His promise to Abraham and to David. Nationally, Israel refused; but we who have received Him have been privileged to enter into all of His promises to David.

Keys represent authority, and authority is power. Jesus has the keys—the authority—the power. He declared boldly at the time of His ascension and the giving of His commission to the Church:

"ALL POWER [Greek, **authority**] is given unto me IN HEAVEN and IN EARTH" (Matthew 28:18).

Just as He had opened the way of truth and holiness to this local church and had retained the power to open and shut at His will, He now assures them (verse 8) that He expects them to go through other doors with the same truth.

CHRIST'S APPRAISAL OF THE CHURCH

"I know thy works: behold, I have set before thee an

open door, and no man can shut it: for thou hast a little strength, and hast kept my word, and hast not denied my name" (Revelation 3:8).

The "open door" refers to verse 7. Christ expressed confidence that the church at Philadelphia would go through that open door. He had forbidden the dissenter to close it.

"Thou hast a little strength"

This church had been tried, but through the struggle, they had "a little strength" left. The Lord is our strength and His store never diminishes. With our trust in Him, we can say with Paul:

"... I take pleasure in infirmities, in reproaches, in necessities, in persecutions, in distresses for Christ's sake: for WHEN I AM WEAK [in self], THEN AM I STRONG [in Christ]" (2 Corinthians 12:10).

It is probable that He had brought them to the point of "little strength" so that they would look to the perpetual Source for that which would be needed to go through the open door without human fear, but in the fear of God. Again, Paul had declared:

"For though we walk in the flesh [fleshly body], we do not war after [in the strength of] the flesh:
"(For the weapons of our warfare are not carnal, but MIGHTY THROUGH GOD to the pulling down of strong holds)" (2 Corinthians 10:3, 4).

Paul's second chapter of First Corinthians is a masterpiece in the awesome contrast between the power and wisdom of men and that of God "in demonstration of the Spirit and of power." (Read the whole chapter carefully at this point.) He encourages implicit faith "in the power of God," which the highest (princes) of earth do not know, or understand.

The Philadelphian saints could confound the Jewish protesters by taking their "little strength" and tapping into "the wisdom of God in a mystery, even the hidden wisdom." And so can we.

"Thou hast kept my word"
Herein lay a large portion of the secret of this church's favor with God. As an old song says, "Little is much if God is in it." And He will be "in it" if we make it our undivided aim to please and glorify Him.

"Better is a little [strength, or whatever] WITH RIGHTEOUSNESS than great revenues without right" (Proverbs 16:8).

"A little that A RIGHTEOUS MAN hath is better than the riches of many wicked" (Psalms 37:16).

Remember the seven loaves and the "FEW LITTLE FISHES" (Matthew 15:34) with which Jesus fed "four thousand men, beside women and children." Remember likewise His promise, "fear not, LITTLE FLOCK; for it is your Father's good pleasure to give you the kingdom" (Luke 12:32); and, "Well, thou good servant: because thou hast been faithful IN A VERY LITTLE, have thou authority over ten cities" (Luke 19:17).

We have "the kingdom" now by faith, and we will have the ultimate "authority," by His appointment, at the end of a sojourn of faithful service. Even though we may have "a very little" at our disposal here, the door is wide open to us if we will faithfully KEEP HIS WORD.

The Philadelphians had first obeyed the Word themselves; then they had guarded it when others were rejecting it. They were faithful, though opposed, defamed, and persecuted. They remembered that "we must through much tribulation enter into the kingdom of God" (Acts 14:22). They remembered that the house of God "is the church of the living God, the pillar and ground of THE TRUTH" (1 Timothy 3:15). They felt responsible to support the truth, to defend it, and to propagate it. In all of these ways they had kept His Word, and now they were being commended.

"Thou hast not denied my name"
They had confessed His name—His Messiahship, His Lordship, His power and authority—stedfastly refusing to deny it even under threats and persecutions, and the constant haranguing from "the synagogue of Satan." In other words,

they had been put to the test and had remained true. Though the Apostle Peter had once denied Him—and later had to repent and be "converted" (Luke 22:31, 32; Mark 16:7)—these saints, possibly having profited from Peter's experience, had not departed from the faith in order to ease their own trials.

THE REWARDS OF FAITHFULNESS

"Behold, I will make them of the synagogue of Satan, which say they are Jews, and are not, but do lie; behold, I will make them to come and worship before thy feet, and to know that I have loved thee.

"Because thou hast kept the word of my patience, I also will keep thee from the hour of temptation [Greek, **trial**], which shall come upon all the world, to try them that dwell upon the earth" (Revelation 3:9, 10).

For the saints' faithfulness under pressure from the lying Jews, He would make those Jews see their error. They would acknowledge that these saints were right, and would come and worship Christ with them. Through it all, they would be convinced of the love He had for these faithful ones at Philadelphia, standing by them and strengthening their resolve to hold fast His name. Undoubtedly many of them were eventually received into fellowship and membership in the church.

How did this come about? We are not told, since it was done later; but from experience in our own day, we know that it was done by the power of God through the Holy Ghost, who bore witness to their hearts by conviction, mellowing them unto confession, genuine repentance, and restitution. The church saints were God's instruments as examples in stedfastness, convincing those Jews that they needed whatever it was that kept them true to Christ's Word and name. God may eventually have brought them down to where they were compelled to examine their own hearts and evil motives.

At any rate, Christ promised this faithful church that, because they had obeyed His Word concerning patience under trial, He would keep them from the prophesied future "hour of temptation"—a time which this world must yet face. It seems apparent that He referred to "the great tribulation" during the era of the Antichrist.

There are diversities of opinion about that period of time, especially relative to the Church, which we feel certain will be raptured before the worst of the tribulation. However, all conjectures together do not do away with Jesus' warning:

"Watch therefore: for ye know not what hour your Lord doth come . . .
"Therefore be ye also ready: for in such an hour as ye think not the Son of man cometh" (Matthew 24:42, 44).

Just suppose the saints should be subjected to the early part of the Antichrist's seven-year limit, when UNPRECEDENTED DECEPTION will seek to overthrow "if it were possible . . . the very elect" (Matthew 24:24). It behooves us to make sure we are so rooted and grounded in the truth and in the faith that we will not be persuaded by a lie. Deception would not be deception if it were easily apparent. While it may be our hope and prayer that the Church will see none of this, it remains our responsibility to warn other souls "to flee from the wrath to come" (Matthew 3:7), who, at this late hour, might well see that awful time!

ADMONITION AND EXHORTATION

"Behold, I come quickly: hold that fast which thou hast, that no man take thy crown" (Revelation 3:11).

Evidently the rapture is intended in this admonition. As was explained in earlier lessons, "quickly" does not necessarily mean "immediately," but suddenly and unexpectedly once the time has come and the event has begun.

The time is in God's power, but any number of things might come our way in the meantime, seeking to deprive us of the crown of life. The gospel records verify the fact that Jesus does not waste words. Therefore, He had good reason to admonish the Philadelphians to hold fast that which they already had, or that to which they had attained. He knew their future. He knew that men tend to grow over-confident and careless when all seems to be going well.

We cannot afford to hold with a loose hand, as it were, such priceless treasures as faith, grace, hope, love, and a holy zeal for God and His Word. Other men cannot take away our crown personally. In fact, we do not possess it as yet. But men can cause us to fail in faith so that we will forfeit the crown we have hoped to obtain. Should we fail, someone else will receive the reward that would have been ours had we remained faithful.

Christ's coming "quickly" will bring judgment upon the evil ones just as truly as He will bring reward to the faithful. In Revelation 2:5 and 16, the admonition is that of impending judgment, while in 3:11 it is a word of encouragement and consolation. The main thought in both is the warning of the awful loss if we are found wanting in the day of judgment.

Now is the time for soul-searching, followed by repentance where it is required, and for continued watchfulness even when all seems well. David comforts the suffering saints in these ways: "... Weeping may endure for a night, but joy cometh in the morning" (Psalms 30:5).

We can live only one day at a time. It takes only one day to fail, but we can "hold fast" day by day also. Paul, being well acquainted with affliction, puts things in the proper perspective:

"For our light affliction, which is but for a moment, worketh for us a far more exceeding and eternal weight of glory;

"While we look not at the things which are seen, but at the things which are not seen: for the things which are seen are temporal; but the things which are not seen are eternal" (2 Corinthians 4:17, 18).

THE PROMISE TO THE OVERCOMER

"Him that overcometh will I make a pillar in the temple of my God, and he shall go no more out: and I will write upon him the name of my God, and the name of the city of my God, which is new Jerusalem, which cometh down out of heaven from my God: and I will write upon him my new name" (Revelation 3:12).

Two opinions vie for acceptance concerning the kind of "pillar" intended here. Both are figurative or symbolic, and both are representative of People:

(1) **The figure of a columnar, supportive pillar**, typical of the large columns that support the super-structure of buildings. Overcomers represent strength, stedfastness, and

endurance. The fact that they have overcome presupposes tests and trials by which they have proven themselves before the Lord. These have supported the truth, both by faith and practice, and have not wavered or compromised.

The periodic earthquakes that had destroyed the heathen temples may have been in the mind of the Lord, and He knew the saints would understand the analogy. The "tremors" of erroneous Jewish persuasions, and perhaps other false teachings which were making the rounds among the seven churches, had not moved this church from the truth. They were a faithful local congregation in the great body of Christ, "the pillar and ground of the truth," and could be depended on for loyal support.

(2) **The figure of a monumental pillar, or marker.** Some hold to this opinion in view of the words that follow, suggesting that the symbolic language is fittingly descriptive of overcomers. In this typical light, the "engravings" might be thought of as a three-fold assurance:

(a) "The name of my God"—the Father of the Lord Jesus Christ, and therefore our God and Father by means of the blessed adoption, making us joint-heirs with Christ (Ephesians 1:6; Romans 8:17), in whom we stand complete (Colossians 2:10). The figure is probably taken from the inscription on the foreheads of the Old Testament priests—"Holiness to the Lord" (Exodus 28:36). The Church is "a royal priesthood" (1 Peter 2:9), and He "hath made us kings and priests unto God . . . and we shall reign on the earth" (Revelation 1:6; 5:10).

Another figure might be that of a seal stamped on His possession, similar to the statement concerning the Holy Ghost wherewith we are sealed as "the earnest of our inheritance unto the redemption of the purchased possession," or "unto the day of redemption" (Ephesians 1:13, 14; 4:30).

(b) "The name of the city of my God, which is new Jerusalem"—apparently referring to our eternal citizenship in the beautiful city which John saw "coming down from God out of heaven, prepared as a bride [the Church] adorned for her husband [Christ]" (Revelation 21:2). Though the Jews had disowned the Philadelphian Christians as unfit for heaven, Jesus overruled them, showing what is the true city of God, and who shall inhabit it (Revelation 21:7, 8, 27).

(c) "My new name"—a name belonging to Christ (Revelation

19:12), whose name we will share. At that point the overcomers will be admitted into His full glory, which now we are incapable of beholding! Even now our lives are "hid with Christ in God" (Colossians 3 :2), and, being His sanctified ones, "He is not ashamed to call [us] brethren" (Hebrews 2:11).

All of these promises intimate the eternal endurance of the Church and her ministry.

LISTENING TO THE LETTER

The Philadelphians Listened

This was a letter of comfort, consolation, and encouragement to an apparently small, struggling church. As we have already seen, their trials sprang from the Jewish element in that city.

While such opposition hounded the Christians everywhere, it appears that the Jews were especially troublesome at Smyrna and Philadelphia. In the letters to both of those churches, Christ spoke of them as being "the synagogue of Satan," saying they were Jews, when they knew they were not so in the spiritual sense. At Smyrna He called it "blasphemy."

Here were two peoples, both claiming the same God, yet appearing to the heathen population as being at war. However, it is not likely that the Christian sector used carnal weapons such as the Jews were using. At any rate, it is abundantly clear that Jesus was pleased with the church's stability and patience in the face of this constant harassment.

How it must have rejoiced their hearts to hear that Christ would eventually constrain those Jews to join them in the worship of the true Messiah, the prophesied Saviour of the world! Even though the struggle might continue awhile, their burden must have been lightened by the assurance that the truth would soon prevail.

Then, their faithfulness to the Word must have contributed something positive to their understanding of His reference to "the hour of temptation." Imagine the peace and joy in hearing that they would be kept from it! He had followed this word of assurance with a mild admonition to hold fast what they now had, and a reminder that they could still fail to receive their crown of victory—the crown of life.

We trust that they were graciously humbled rather than

egotistically exalted at hearing the Master's promises to "him that overcometh." The singular "him" and "he" spoke to each member as an individual, being used four times in verse 12, and twice more in the conclusion:

"He that hath ears to hear, let him hear what the Spirit saith unto the churches."

Are WE Listening?

Does the Philadelphian letter portray the possibility of a perfect Church? If so, we must understand that the mark will not be reached without opposition. Some of the other churches were plagued by internal problems. The church at Philadelphia was hindered by an outside enemy who pledged something of a "lying allegiance" to the same God. No doubt the Jews posed two problems: (1) They hindered the evangelical efforts of this church among the heathen prospects, and (2) they were incessantly trying to persuade the members to defect.

Are we listening? We rightly bemoan Church deterioration "from within." But we do have a scriptural government by which we can master internal difficulties, if we will operate it. Does Satan use our neglect in this area to hinder normal growth?

On the "outside" is a multitude of "uncertain sounds" —conflicting interpretations of the faith and doctrine—each with a considerable "following," all singing, "Praise God from whom all blessings flow!"—all crying, "Lord! Lord!" and all "in Jesus' name"! Internal problems that are allowed to remain problems, and which foster more and greater problems, tend to make those outside "uncertain sounds" seem attractive to a weary membership!

Are we still listening to Christ's commendation of the church at Philadelphia? They had kept His Word—and the Word must be KNOWN if it is to be KEPT. They had not denied His name—were not ashamed of the name "Christian" and "Church of God."

In current vernacular, would Jesus say to us, "You have kept your avowed obligation to accept the Bible rightly divided as the Word of God"? Would He say, "You have not denied in name, faith, or practice, the Church of God which I purchased with my own blood"?

Christ's "voice" while in this world repeatedly clashed with the "uncertain sounds" around Him. He openly declared:

"Think not that I am come to send peace on earth: I came not to send peace, but a sword.

"For I am come to set a man at variance against his father, and the daughter against her mother, and the daughter in law against her mother in law.

"And a man's foes shall be they of his own household.

"He that loveth father or mother more than me is not worthy of me: and he that loveth son or daughter more than me is not worthy of me.

"And he that taketh not his cross, and followeth after me is not worthy of me.

"He that findeth his life shall lose it: and he that loseth his life for my sake shall find it" (Matthew 10:34-39).

There should be no divisions in the Church, which is to come to the unity of the faith (Ephesians 4:3, 13). But we are not to be in unity with the world, even if those of our family become our foes. Sectarian differences often cause division. But Christ is "true." He is "the truth." If we would be worthy of Him, He must have first place in our hearts.

When we attempt to fellowship in "ecumenical circles," do we make the Church's voice to be heard in the promotion of sound doctrine? Or are we silenced by accusations of causing division? Does the oft-touted "fellowship" remain intact when we declare what we mean by "one Church for all"?

Jesus was bold to say to those Jews who sought to tempt Him: "From the beginning it was not so" (Matthew 19:8); "Ye have heard . . . but I say unto you . . . " (Matthew 5:21, 22, 27, 28, 38, 39).

The truth still brings division because this world is rarely a friend to God's truth. The question is: Are we good Philadelphians, refusing to compromise Christ's Word and name, even though the opposition wears us down to only "a little strength"? Are we willing in this day of professed "unity of all Christians" to identify with the real, biblical Jesus, who said:

"Blessed are ye, when men shall hate you, and when they shall separate you from their company, and shall reproach you, and cast out your name as evil, FOR THE SON OF MAN'S SAKE" (Luke 6:22).

Like Jesus and the apostles, we must go where men are in order to spread the gospel. Then, when God gives us "an open door," we must make use of the opportunity to proclaim the Word of truth as it was from the beginning. He who holds "the key" may not open that same door to us again.

"He that hath an ear to hear, let him hear . . . ."

—Lesson 9—

THE CHURCH AT LAODICEA

RELATION OF CITY AND CHURCH

The Geographical, Cultural, and Historical Situation

Geography: Laodicea, in the district of Phrygia, was situated in the valley of the Lycos River, which was a tributary of the larger Maeander River less than twenty miles to the north. The city was at the juncture of three trade routes. One connected Laodicea with the Roman Post Road at Philadelphia fifty miles to the northeast, and another led from the east to Ephesus, about a hundred twenty-five miles to the west. The city of Colosse (now Honaz) was about fifteen miles to the east.

Laodicea was built on seven hills, like Rome. It was a very wealthy and prosperous commercial and industrial city. Its trade consisted of gold from the river's sands; a glossy black wool, from which was made cloaks, blankets, and carpets; and the manufacture of medical drugs, especially an eye salve known as Phrygian powder, or collyrium. It was also an important banking center.

Culture and History: The **Thompson Bible Survey** gives the following information: "Laodicea was one of those towns in the Neolithic period (following the Old Stone Age) characterized by new sources of food supply and the development of pottery and weaving. Historical references begin with the ancient name of Diaspolis [city of Zeus] and Rhoas. The Hellenistic ruler, Antiochus II [King of Persia] (261-246 B.C.), rebuilt and renamed the city after his sister-wife, Laodice. **Josephus** says that his successor, Antiochus III (223-187 B.C.), brought in Jewish settlers to Laodicea "from Syria and Babylon . . . ."

About thirty years before John sent the "revelation" letter, Laodicea had been destroyed by an earthquake, but the wealthy—and possibly arrogant—city declined Rome's offer of financial assistance in the rebuilding process. Apparently the city already felt—as the church did later—that they "had need of nothing" from any source outside themselves.

As for "religion," there were the pagan gods, principally centering around the Temple of Zeus. The church at Laodicea is thought to have been established by Epaphras, apparently an associate of Paul's. (See Colossians 4:12-15.) As in other places, there may have been Jews at Laodicea who were present in Jerusalem at the Feast of Pentecost in A.D. 33, and were converted by Peter's preaching.

Even after John's day, the church at Laodicea had a long history. According to the **Pulpit Commentary** and the **Thompson Bible Survey**, Laodicea had representation at the Council of Nicea in A.D. 325, and the general Church Council of Laodicea was held there in A.D. 361. Then, in A.D. 449, Laodicea's Bishop Nunechius II participated in a Church Council at Ephesus. It must be remembered, of course, that the last two dates were in the period now known as the Dark Ages of Church history.

The **Thompson Bible Survey** says: "The wealth and worldly prestige led to an increased licentiousness and compromise on moral issues ....The church adopted a spirit of accommodation and of broad toleration, and was entirely self-satisfied. Proud of its prestige in the city, of its apostate tradition, of its generosity and wealth, it had 'need of nothing' in its own eyes."

Today, the ruins of the old city surround a village named Eski-Hissar. The modern city of Denizli, more or less taking Laodicea's place, lies a few miles to the south.

CHRIST INTRODUCES HIMSELF

> "And unto the angel of the church of the Laodiceans write; These things saith the Amen, the faithful and true witness, the beginning of the creation of God" (Revelation 3:14).

Historical records offer an interesting possibility, at least, about "the angel," or pastor, of the Laodicean Church. In Colossians 4:15-17 and Philemon 2, one by the name of Archippus is introduced. One source, "The Apostolical Constitutions," asserts that Archippus was "first Bishop of Laodicea." Paul counted him "our fellowsoldier"—that is, a fellowsoldier with himself and Philemon. It is suggested that Archippus may have been the son of the well-to-do Philemon, living at Colosse, and pastoring the church at Laodicea some six or eight miles to the east. It is further conjectured, from Paul's admonition to him "to take heed to the ministry," that his own comfort and ease was reflected in the "have need of nothing" attitude of that church. All of this has to assume a very long pastorate if he was still pastor there some thirty-five years after Paul's letters to Colosse and Philemon. However, a man's influence may linger for many years after his departure.

"The Amen, the faithful and true witness"

Some grammarians think the two expressions, "Amen" and "faithful and true witness," are in opposition—both meaning the same, but explaining one another.

"Amen" variously means: "so be it"; "truly"; "certainly"; "verily"; or "I approve"—depending on the context. It is used here as one of the proper names for Christ, and testifies to His faithfulness and truth with emphatic positiveness. It was with this intent that He had so often said while on earth, "Verily, verily, I say unto you . . . "; "Truly, truly, I am saying this . . . ."

As He had said to the Philadelphians—"he that is true"—so says He here. What He would be saying was like "the last word" to a church in serious trouble. As the great "AMEN," His promise, either of good or ill, was with authority of fulfillment. A fitting complement to Christ as "the Amen" is found in 2 Corinthians 1:18-20:

> "But as God is true, our word toward you was not yea and nay.
> "For the Son of God, Jesus Christ, who was preached among you by us . . . was not yea and nay, but in him was yea.
> "For all the promises of God in him are yea, and in him Amen, unto the glory of God by us."

Apparently Paul's reason for not having visited the church at Corinth had been misunderstood. Here he assures them that he had not used "lightness" (verse 17)—fickleness, or double-talk, indicating that he would not stoop to such an abuse of the example of Christ. With Him, or IN HIM, yea is yea forever, and nay is nay forever. So it was with Paul, and so it should be with us, making it unnecessary to seal our word with an oath (Matthew 5:33-37).

IN CHRIST we have ALL FULFILLMENT, even to the last

jot and tittle of the law (Matthew 5:17, 18). The promises are true and their fulfillment [the end, or Amen] is sure, in themselves giving proof of their authenticity.

Thus, this "church of the Laodiceans" would be hearing no empty threats. THIS WAS IT! The AMEN! Would they take heed? In effect, Christ was saying, "I come to undeceive you; to draw back the curtain and show you Myself as the truth, which, in turn, should show you the truth about your own nauseating condition!"

As "faithful," He is worthy of being believed and trusted "on His record," as it were. Thus, His witness is true. He was faithful to the Father, who appointed Him as our great High Priest (Hebrews 3:1, 2), and He is faithful "as a son over his own house; whose house are we, if we hold fast the confidence [the assurance of our salvation] and the rejoicing of our hope [of eternal life] firm unto the end" (Hebrews 3:6).

As the "true witness," His witness to men was true, even if not accepted, and His witness about men to His Father would be true and accepted (Matthew 10:32, 33). In Malachi 3:5, God was "a swift witness" against the sorcerers, adulterers, false swearers, oppressors of hired servants, the fatherless, and those who showed bias to strangers; but at Laodicea, His witness is against a seemingly prosperous, contented, peaceful people. From His omniscient vantage point, Christ saw the Laodiceans as they really were, not as they thought they were. As God's TRUE WITNESS, (1) He had absolute knowledge of the facts—not mere "circumstantial evidence"; and (2) He was above all temptation to misrepresent—to be bribed to defend the wrong!

"The beginning of the creation of God"

In the overall context of the Scriptures—"the volume of the book" (Psalms 40:7; Hebrews 10:7; John 5:39)—it is clear that Christ is God the Son, every whit as divine as God the Father and God the Holy Ghost. Since this is true, Christ was not "created."

Look closely at John 1, verses 1, 2 and 14. In the beginning, Christ WAS. Since He WAS, He was not created; no more so than the Holy Ghost was created. The Divine Son was "MADE FLESH"—"a little lower than the angels for the suffering of death" (Hebrews 2:9)—because depraved man needed a PERFECT SACRIFICE who could redeem him from

Adam's fall. Jesus was that Perfect Sacrifice. Thus, He became the Son of man without abdicating His deity as the Son of God.

Paul describes Him as "the image of the invisible God, the firstborn of every creature . . . who is the beginning, the firstborn from the dead" (Colossians 1:15, 18). He is the "firstborn" creature that has risen "from the dead" in immortality—nevermore to die—"the firstfruits of them that slept" (1 Corinthians 15:20).

The original text indicates that "the beginning of the creation of God" means "the original Source" of God's work of creation. This is substantiated by Paul's verities—

"For BY HIM were ALL THINGS created . . . ALL THINGS were created BY HIM, and FOR HIM:

"And he IS BEFORE ALL THINGS, and BY HIM all things consist [have substance and cohere]" (Colossians 1:16, 17).

Again, John says, "ALL THINGS were made BY HIM; and without him was not ANY THING made that was made" (John 1:3).

Another commentator says that our text means that Christ was "the moving cause of the creation of God."

The Laodiceans probably were not concerned about all the "possible meanings." In their more fervent days, they had known Him for who He is and what He is. Now, their concern was to hear what He would be saying to them in their letter sent to them by John.

CHRIST'S APPRAISAL OF THE CHURCH

"I know thy works, that thou art neither cold nor hot: I would thou wert cold or hot. So then because thou art lukewarm, and neither cold nor hot, I will spue thee out of my mouth.

"Because thou sayest, I am rich, and increased with goods, and have need of nothing; and knowest not that thou art wretched, and miserable, and poor, and blind, and naked" (Revelation 3:15, 16).

The Indictment

The above appraisal is a somewhat baffling indictment. It

has been suggested that Jesus used the word "lukewarm" because He knew that people would immediately grasp His analytical meaning from the tepid water with which they were familiar. Laodicea's water supply came by conduit from Hierapolis on the Maeander River about ten miles to the northeast. The residents loathed the soda-laden water, which was so lukewarm when it reached them that it often caused vomiting. From this figure they would understand that the form and manner of their church affairs were so nauseating to Christ that He was about to vomit them out! Be that as it may, we will explore some of the implications in Christ's words as to the possible meaning of "lukewarmness" in the context of His indictment.

The Laodicean Rebuke: It is reasonable to assume that His will was that they be HOT—"on fire for God," we may say. This could mean being spiritually zealous, eager, passionate, ardent, enthusiastic, in humble, unpretentious, sincere and dedicated worship and service for God. He could have borne with them had they been COLD—without warm affection for God and spiritual things; not yet interested in salvation; totally indifferent to a godly lifestyle. But LUKEWARMNESS—a disgusting blend of devotion and apathy; of lip-service and works-denial—these were reprehensible; totally unacceptable! Surely they knew that He had said:

"If any man come to me, and hate not [comparatively] his father, and mother, and wife, and children, and brethren, and sisters, yea, and his own life also, he cannot be my disciple.

"And whosoever doth not bear his cross, and come after me, cannot be my disciple" (Luke 14:26, 27).

Recognizing Lukewarmness: Just how qualified are men to judge a church, or an individual, as being "lukewarm"? What criteria are we to use? How are we to know if we are using the same criteria that Jesus used in His view of Laodicea? Since lukewarmness is essentially the opposite of spirituality, any suggested "norms" would vary—perhaps widely.

For example: Brother A and Brother B are traveling together. They stop at Laodicea for service. Brother A struggles to stay awake. Brother B enjoys every minute of the service. They go on to Sardis. Brother A shouts loud and long with this church that has a name that is "liveth." Brother B is not favorably impressed. Since we know what the record says about both churches, we conclude that neither Brother A nor Brother B is right in his appraisal. Brother A sensed Laodicea's lukewarmness while Brother B did not. At Sardis Brother A did not realize that their "liveliness" was only a matter of keeping alive "a name" earned by an earlier generation of saints, while Brother B was the one to sense the spirit of "vain show."

Spirituality is not necessarily in "bodily exercise" (1 Timothy 4:8) or an activity-packed program, though these may be present in a truly spiritual church. **Lukewarmness**, on the other hand, does not necessarily mean relative quietness and little outward evidence of good works, though these may be true of a really lukewarm church. Individual personalities and personal likes and dislikes make it unwise to use such things as an ironclad criterion for either spirituality or lukewarmness. So we must search deeper, praying for spiritual discernment and sound, righteous judgment before likening this-or-that church, or individual member, to Laodicea and its members.

Possible Evidences and Causes of Lukewarmness

The Cause Peculiar to Laodicea: We can derive at least a glimmering of the cause of Laodicea's problem from their own boastings and the evident unawareness or ignorance of their spiritual state in the Lord's sight (verse 17). His true evaluation was directly the opposite of what they were saying of themselves—"I am rich, and increased with goods, and have need of nothing." But this proud confession pinpointed the root cause of their indictment.

Raymond M. Pruitt, in the "Sunday School Teacher's Commentary," Lesson 9, for April 26, 1987, has given an exposition of the Laodicean situation as it would, in all probability, apply to a similar church today:

> The wealth of Laodicea was a fundamental factor in their lack of moral and spiritual fervor. There is no indication that the church was disturbed by internal heresies, or scarred by persecution. Its coffers were full;

there was no problem with meeting the bills; its members were comfortable. The services were held without strain; nobody in the church had a contentious spirit; everybody had paid his annual obligation; the preacher was being well-supported, had a nice parsonage well furnished. They led all other churches in giving; attendance was good, new people were coming every week; everybody was well pleased with their pastor, and with their church. No problems. **Yet wait!** There were serious problems. It was just that nobody recognized that the church had fallen into a stupor of spiritual death, and was ready to expire.

. . . This church had deluded itself into thinking that it was on firm footing. Similar to many churches today, they had material prosperity; they were involved with impressive projects which cost a lot of money. They could afford the best. Yet they had no real love for Christ, and were indifferent to the needs of the lost and the destitute around them. Such churches may point to their impressive buildings and their large, modern parsonages, and say, "Look how God has blessed us!" However, material things have zero value in the spiritual realm. The rich fool of Luke 19:16-21 learned that lesson to his great sorrow.

(NOTE: Review this subject in Lesson Four of this course, under "Endurance in Proverty.")

Other Possible Current Considerations: (1) **A church membership syndrome:** With the passing of generations and changes in the social and economic situation, the church membership almost certainly will be affected. If it becomes too numbers-conscious, or too finance-conscious, there will be the temptation to avoid teaching and preaching sound Bible doctrine and the maintenance of the Church's original stand on that doctrine, in order to attract an element who would not be candidates for membership on those grounds.

If the "changed life," the sanctified life, and the Spirit-filled life are given the compromised "light touch," in a surprisingly short time the church roll can become loaded with non-spiritual members, and professing members who have never experienced the new birth, in the Spirit. (NOTE: See Lesson Seven, "Empty professions of faith.") An appealing "program," along with "exciting" competitive projects and civic involvements, may result in impressive growth and satisfying publicity—and a spiritual lukewarmness that makes God sick!

(2) **An education obsession:** In an era when higher and higher education seems mandatory by a privileged society, this advanced learning can be abused by misuse.

In turn, the Holy Ghost can be abused by being largely ignored as to His God-given office as stated by Jesus: (a) as "the Spirit of truth; whom the world [educated or not] cannot receive" (John 14:17); (b) as He who "shall teach you all things" (John 14:26); (c) as "the Spirit of truth" who bears witness and testifies of Christ (John 15:26, 27); (d) as "the Spirit of truth" who guides into "all truth" and shows things to come (John 16:13); (e) as the One who gives the power for truly effective witnessing for Christ (Acts 1:8); (f) as the One who gives preachers and preaching the necessary "demonstration of the Spirit and of power" (1 Corinthians 2:4); and (g) as He who searches and reveals "the deep things of God" (1 Corinthians 2:10), "not in the words which man's wisdom [education] teacheth, but which the Holy Ghost teacheth" (1 Corinthians 2:13).

The Apostle Paul was as exceptionally well-educated man in his day, and there is no better example than his of the proper relationship in which he held his learning with respect to the all-wise, all-knowing Spirit of God.

The Apostles Peter and John, and perhaps the others, were considered "unlearned and ignorant men" by those on the Sanhedrin Council (Acts 4:13); but those same councilmen marvelled at their powerful preaching and knowledge of the Word.

When a church allows education to become an obsession, **requiring** its ministers to be "degree men," elevating human wisdom and knowledge above that of God, and considering the less educated members inferior in their ability to conduct the spiritual and business matters, that church will become lukewarm despite all efforts and contention to the contrary. It may "bless itself" momentarily, but God will soon leave it to its own preferred devices.

(NOTE: See the remarks on this subject in Lesson Three.)

(3) **Love of the things of the world:** Jesus warned His disciples of the world's hatred and persecution:

"If the world hate you, ye know that it hated me before it hated you.

"If ye were of the world, the world would love his own: but because ye are not of the world, but I have chosen you out of the world, therefore the world hateth you" (John 15:18, 19).

His frank exposure of men's sins made them hate Him. The same effect will result when we boldly expose sin and the sinner's hell. We can withhold these truths and the world will take us unto its bosom for its own advantage. We may enjoy the "strained peace" when we actually should be suffering conviction for our abominable spirit of compromise.

James forthrightly declares, "... Whosoever therefore will be a friend of the world is the enemy of God" (James 4:4). He spoke this in the context of adultery, but if idolatry is spiritual adultery, so is friendship with the world. The world becomes a "god" that stands between us and the true and living God.

A church that loves the world's fellowship and takes up its lifestyles and practices becomes God's enemy, and whatever "fire" that church may seem to have will be of its own kindling.

There has probably never been a generation that has not wrestled with the plague of worldliness. All too often the "liberals" have out-talked or turned a deaf ear to the "conservatives," and have prevailed. A little more of the world's ways, "things," and philosophies have been passed on to succeeding generations, who "inherit" them as being acceptable.

A loose rein on worldliness leaves it free to send its roots deeper and deeper, penetrating even the most sacred fundamental doctrines of Christ and His Church, and diluting their profound truths. A church that has learned to "sin and shout" is an enemy of God. Its lukewarmness has become comfortable to the membership, who "KNOWEST NOT" that they are "wretched, and miserable, and poor, and blind, and naked" in the eyes of God.

(4) **A legalistic preoccupation with orthodoxy:** Orthodoxy simply means conformity to the usual beliefs or established doctrines of one's religion. We are expected to respect and abide by the established doctrines of the Church, which we

hold to because they are Bible doctrine. But when doctrine becomes a preoccupation to the extent that the spirit of love and grace is overridden by the legalistic spirit of the law, joyful obedience is lost and a mechanical kowtowing to threats of discipline and judgment takes its place.

Christ completely fulfilled the law, not by destroying it, but by perfectly keeping it in our behalf. Read it in His own words:

> "Think not that I am come to destroy the law, or the prophets: I am not come to destroy, but to fulfil.
>
> "For verily I say unto you, Till heaven and earth pass, one jot or one tittle shall in no wise pass from the law, till all be fulfilled.
>
> "Whosoever therefore shall break one of these least commandments, and shall teach men so, he shall be called the least in the kingdom of heaven: but whosoever shall do and teach them, the same shall be called great in the kingdom of heaven.
>
> "For I say unto you, That except your righteousness shall exceed the righteousness of the scribes and Pharisees, ye shall in no case enter into the kingdom of heaven" (Matthew 5:17-20).

GOD SO LOVED US that He gave His Son for the purpose of keeping the law in the spirit of grace. In suffering or satisfying our sin penalty, He let us go free. Then, that LOVE is shed abroad in our hearts by the Holy Ghost (Romans 5:5). Now we in turn love the One who set us free from death; and we also love the law that, through His love, enables us to obey it with joyful willingness. In this lies the great truth of the Gospel. Jesus, on another occasion, said it very simply:

> "And ye shall know the truth, and the truth shall make you free" (John 8:32).

He who professes faith in Christ, yet is offended by the requirements of His Word, his profession is an empty one. He has not been set free. He is yet in his sins.

It would appear, then, that those who administer the Word in the spirit of the unfulfilled law are themselves in the bondage of a wretched legalism. They need the blessed deliverance which the once-wretched Paul received after coming to grips with his unsanctified state.

"O wretched man that I am! who shall deliver me from the body of this death?
"I thank God through Jesus Christ our Lord..." (Romans 7:24, 25).

So—a legalistic "angel," or "pastor," who imposes his preoccupation with an unbending orthodoxy on the membership, will have a lukewarm church, for legalism tends to quench the fire of love, truth, and grace.

Miscellaneous Causes: The list could go on and on, overlapping here and there, perhaps: (a) **Egotism** can destroy a church and every soul in it. Self-righteousness; self-justification; self-exaltation; self-indulgence; self-satisfaction—all are related to secular humanism, or "self-godism." They result in damning self-destruction! (b) **A mistaken idea of "blessings,"** closely related to egotism. God's blessings, when abused and misused, or squandered, can be turned into a curse, producing a very formal, complacent church. (c) **Misplaced priorities**—cares of this life instead of soul-burden; outward show of prosperity instead of soul prosperity and a wealth of souls won to Christ; all emotional "worship" instead of worshipful service to those in need of help, spiritually or otherwise.

ADMONITION, EXHORTATION, AND CONSEQUENCES

"I counsel thee to buy of me gold tried in the fire, that thou mayest be rich; and white raiment, that thou mayest be clothed, and that the shame of thy nakedness do not appear; and anoint thine eyes with eye-salve, that thou mayest see.
"As many as I love, I rebuke and chasten: be zealous therefore, and repent" (Revelation 3:18, 19).

The Change
(1) **Receive Counsel:** Despite their sickening condition, Christ loved them; and because He loved them so much, He rebuked and chastened them, lest they continue in a way that would work their eternal doom. Upon hearing these words,

perhaps they recalled a similar message from the Epistle to the Hebrews:

Epistle to the Hebrews:

" ... My son, despise not thou the chastening of the Lord, nor faint when thou art rebuked of him:

"For whom the Lord loveth he chasteneth, and scourgeth every son whom he receiveth.

"If ye endure chastening, God dealeth with you as with sons; for what son is he whom the father chasteneth not?

. . .

"Now no chastening for the present seemeth to be joyous, but grievous: nevertheless afterward it yieldeth the peaceable fruit of righteousness unto them which are exercised thereby" (Hebrews 12:5-7, 11).

He counselled the Laodiceans. Counsel may be accepted or rejected, but He would extend to them the opportunity to correct their condition.

Christ, the Source of Every Resource: They had said, "We are rich." He said, "You know not that you are poor." Now He adds, "Buy of ME gold tried in the fire, that thou mayest BE rich." The riches they had were pitifully perishable. He had "the true riches"—"the unsearchable riches of Christ," which was the Gospel of the grace of God to all who would believe (Ephesians 3:8). The prophet had foretold it in these words:

"Ho, every one that thirsteth, come ye to the waters, and he that hath no money; come ye, buy, and eat; yea, come, buy wine and milk without money and without price.

"Wherefore do ye spend money for that which is not bread? and your labour for that which satisfieth not? hearken diligently unto me, and eat ye that which is good, and let your soul delight itself in fatness" (Isaiah 55:1, 2).

Perhaps Christ would subject this church to a trial of their faith, for Peter had said: "That the trial of your faith, being MUCH MORE PRECIOUS THAN OF GOLD that perisheth, though it be tried with fire, might be found unto praise and honour and glory at the appearing of Jesus Christ" (1 Peter 1:7).

They had said, "We are increased with goods, and have need of nothing." Jesus said, "You are wretched, miserable, blind, and naked." Now He adds, "Buy of me white raiment, that ye may be clothed, and that the shame of thy nakedness do not appear." The white raiment always refers to the righteousness of God (Isaiah 1:18; Daniel 7:9; Mark 9:3); the imputed righteousness of faith (Romans 4:3-8; Philippians 3:9); or "the righteousness of saints: which they have received of God (Revelation 7:14; 19:8). Though formally professing to be Christians, Jesus knew they were trusting in their own works—their own self-sufficiency. If necessary, He would pronounce them "cold"; perhaps even unsaved. Like a sudden splash of cold water, perhaps they could be made to respond to His counsel. In their present lukewarmness, they could scarcely be moved.

He would have then exchanged their "fig leaves" of self-righteousness for the blood-sacrifice covering of the Lamb "slain from the foundation of the world" (Revelation 13:8; 1 Peter 1:20). Their nakedness represented their sinful state which could not be hidden from God;

> "Neither is there any creature that is not manifest in his sight: but all things are naked and opened unto the eyes of him with whom we have to do" (Hebrews 4:13).

He counselled them to cover their sin with the love-covering of Christ's efficacious sacrifice (1 Peter 4:8).

For their blindness, He counselled them to "anoint thine eyes with eyesalve, that thou mayest see." He probably alluded to the medical eyesalve which was manufactured in Laodicea. Some of the members of the church may have been employed there. Of course, that eyesalve was effective only if applied. Jesus was saying, "I am offering you spiritual eyesight. If you would see, you must apply the remedy I offer." He had told Nicodemus that "Except a man be born again, he cannot SEE the kingdom of God" (John 3:3). The Laodiceans needed this new birth, or at least a renewal of their earlier experience. They were blind to their need. As Peter had written, they were so lacking in the spiritual virtues that they had forgotten the time when they were "purged from [their] old sins" (2 Peter 1:9), if indeed they ever had been.

(2) **Be zealous:** Their lukewarmness indicated no zeal for Christ and His cause. If they were in a backslidden condition, they were still not necessarily stupid. They could pray if they would. They could confess that Christ's appraisal of their situation was accurate. In other words, they had been warned. The next move was theirs.

(3) **Repent:** Confession that falls short of repentance and turning from their sins unto God would be profitless. It would only increase their guilt. There would have to be some humbling of themselves, then some practical effort to change their ways from a lifestyle of ease to one of presenting themselves "a living sacrifice, holy, acceptable unto God" (Romans 12:1, 2). This was only a "reasonable service," but it would require a severance from conformity with the world, and a transformation by the renewing of their minds. Only by this route would they be able to prove that they were willing to do "that good, and acceptable, and perfect will of God."

The Consequences

Unless they accepted the proffered counsel, and became zealous unto repentance, Christ would follow through on His earlier declaration—"I will spue thee out of my mouth." This apparently meant that He would expel them from His presence; separate them from Himself as being unworthy of His continued longsuffering, even though He would love them unto the end. This expulsion seems to mean an immediate judgment pertaining to that local church's continuance of discontinuance.

A Final Invitation

> "Behold, I stand at the door, and knock: if any man hear my voice, and open the door, I will come in to him, and will sup with him, and he with me" (Revelation 3:20).

Here we see Christ's loving reluctance to leave this church in its present lost condition. But He was outside. He would not intrude unwanted. He knocked on the door, and called to those inside, hoping that someone would hear His voice and open unto Him. He longed for mutual communion—to sup together with them.

Man's free will is clearly evidenced here. Though He pled with them as a local body, the call was also to "any man." He would sup with "him." One man's positive response might result in many more doing likewise. It was a tense moment; then the letter continued.

THE PROMISE TO THE OVERCOMER

"To him that overcometh will I grant to sit with me in my throne, even as I also overcame, and am set down with my Father in his throne" (Revelation 3:21).

Only God—in this instance, God the Son—is capable of such incomprehensible condescension! Here was a church which had fallen into such a state of disgust as to be worthy only of utter expulsion from before God's face. Yet, if they would only "open the door" and give Him His opportunity—if they would submit to His holy counsel—if they would repent of those things which had made them "lukewarm" and repulsive—if they would bring themselves into a state of true devotional and loving obedience—all the past would be blotted out and they would share in Christ's glory!

Of course, it is not just the Laodicean saints who will share His throne. All of the redeemed who endure to the end will rule and reign with Him (Revelation 20:4, 6). But there are times when the individual church, or the individual believer, needs the comfort of reassurance.

He says "IN my throne," not "ON my throne." Possibly this means the peculiar relationship which the Church has with Christ. We are IN HIM. Paul says, "For we are members of his body, of his flesh, and of his bones" (Ephesians 5:30). We are "joint-heirs with Christ" (Romans 8:17). Paul likens the "one flesh" relationship of man and wife to that of Christ and His Church. He says it is a "great mystery" (Ephesians 5:32). This is a closeness such as only God can effect.

At this time Christ, by virtue of His having overcome in His own behalf and ours, sits with His Father in the Father's throne. But He has been promised His own throne—"the throne of his father David" (Isaiah 9:6, 7; Luke 1:32). This refers to the Millennial Reign, which will follow the rapture and "the marriage of the Lamb" (Revelation 19:7). It is then that the Church will share in His reign—IN HIS THRONE! Hallelujah!

LISTENING TO THE LETTER

"He that hath an ear, let him hear what the Spirit saith unto the churches" (Revelation 3:22).

Laodicea Listened

Imagine this lukewarm congregation gathered to hear the reading of a letter from Christ. When the announcement had gone out, it was probably heard with apathetic indifference. For most of them, "Christ" was only a name with some sort of mystical significance. But, being "traditional church-goers," and out of curiosity, they came to hear.

Did His introduction of Himself command better attention? Mere scholastic intelligence would have enabled them to sense "the unusual:" in His words—"the Amen, the faithful and true witness, the beginning of the creation of God." Certainly Christ knew them, and He would not have spoken, or written, "over their heads." The pastor had undoubtedly given the letter a pre-reading. Perhaps he had slept very little in the meantime. We would suppose that he read slowly, in the interest of his hearers' concentration.

While they were still praying to comprehend the introduction, they were jolted to even closer attention by His frank and shocking appraisal of their condition! Reactions may have varied. After all, few, if any, were "spiritual" (in Paul's language—1 Corinthians 3:1). "Carnal" may have applied to some, but "natural" probably covered the majority.

Since "the Spirit" also was speaking (verse 22), we like to think that conviction fell upon them early in the reading, and that, in the secrecy of their hearts at least, they were confessing to the truth of His indictment. We want to believe that the assurance of His love, despite the rebuke and chastening (verse 19), mellowed their hearts unto genuine, tearful life-changing repentance.

We sincerely trust that they heard His knock and invited Him in and that the communion was glorious! If so, "the church of the Laodiceans" was a very different people henceforth.

Are WE Listening?

It is truly appalling that a church's opinion of itself could be so totally opposite the Lord's true knowledge of the church! The same is true of the individual's estimate of himself. And the church is made up of individuals—"members in particular" (1 Corinthians 12:27).

In light of the coming together of GOD'S GREAT MERCY and His AWFUL JUSTICE on Calvary, it is little wonder that a lukewarm church is nauseating to the Christ who suffered there!

We ask, "Did Laodicea listen? Did they repent? Did they let Christ in?"

Are WE listening? Is He knocking at OUR door?

We wonder—If they accepted His counsel, just how did they go about responding to it? They seemed so completely "out of touch." What route might they have taken to recovery?

How would WE respond? Would we begin by "scheduling a revival"? If so, could we be sure we were not "scheduling" a lukewarm evangelist? Would we count him as "on fire" because he preached fast and loud? moved rapidly? spoke much in tongues? flambuoyantly kept the congregation "on their feet" applauding and shouting?

Perhaps it would be better to "hear what the Spirit SAITH" —remembering that the Holy Ghost neither SAYS nor DOES anything contrary to the inspired, infallible, "settled in heaven" Word of God.

Would we start with prayer meetings, beginning with the family altar?

Would we immediately encourage Bible study? If so, who would direct or teach, considering the repugnant apathy toward truth which had prevailed for too long? Could we be sure that the "have need of nothing" spirit of intellectualism had been crucified, giving the Holy Ghost His freedom to "teach" and "guide" and reveal "the deep things of God"?

Emerging from an extended period of spiritual formality, complacency, and self-determinism would be the opportune time to follow Paul's advice to the philosophical Athenians:

"That they should SEEK THE LORD, if haply they

might FEEL AFTER HIM, and FIND HIM, though he be not far from every one of us" (Acts 17:27).

Are we listening? Remember that the Laodiceans were on the verge of being "spued out," but Christ still loved them. He was still knocking—perhaps weeping. Do we really comprehend His merciful compassion? Lyricist **C. Bishop** has expressed his wonder and amazement in the old hymn entitled "Such Love":

> That God should love a sinner such as I,
> Should yearn to change my sorrow into bliss;
> or rest till He had planned to bring me nigh—
> HOW WONDERFUL IS LOVE LIKE THIS!
>   Such love! Such wondrous love!
>   Such love! Such wondrous love!
>   That God should love a sinner such as I—
>   HOW WONDERFUL IS LOVE LIKE THIS!
>   HALLELUJAH! AMEN!

—Lesson Ten—
POSTVIEW AND SUMMATION

Revelation, chapters 2 and 3 answer to Christ's reference in 1:19 to "the things which ARE." The letters were to seven local churches then in existence. We have said before that the total content of those letters speaks to the Church today, and their message will continue to be pertinent as long as the Church remains on earth, or until it is caught up at Christ's second coming.

It is to be noted that the word "church" is not used again beyond chapter 3 until the last chapter, verses 16 and 17. There Christ reverts to "the things which are," once again mentioning His testimony to the churches, and extending an invitation by "the Spirit and the bride [the Church]" to come and "take the water of life freely."

Beginning with chapter 4, He deals with "things which shall be HEREAFTER" (1:19). John is called away from the earth to heaven, from where he will behold certain things there, as well as those events which are to take place on this earth during the closing years of this present age. References which apparently involve the Church beyond the rapture are noted in a few instances, particularly: (1) In 7:9-17, where a numberless multitude of the redeemed is in view, thought by many to be the raptured Church, though others entertain the possibility that they are those who will give their lives during the great tribulation rather than take the mark of the beast; (2) in 19:7, where "his wife" certainly means the Church; and (3) in 21:2, where the new Jerusalem is presented "as a bride adorned for her husband." (Analytically, the inhabitants give meaning to "the city.")

Chapters 4 through 22 relate coming events which are definitely a part of the Church's responsibility to declare now, lest billions of unwary souls are caught unprepared—unsaved, and remain in this tribulation-bound world during the demonic seven-year reign of the beast—the Antichrist. But the Church will be unqualified to discharge its ministerial responsibility if the warnings, admonitions, commendations, and promises contained in the seven letters are slighted or ignored.

John F. Walvoord alerts us to seven "dangers" of which

we are warned in these messages: (1) The danger of losing our first love (Ephesus); (2) the danger of fear of suffering (Smyrna); (3) the constant danger of doctrinal compromise (Pergamos); (4) the danger of moral compromise (Thyatira); (5) the danger of spiritual deadness (Sardis); (6) the danger of not holding fast what "little strength" we may have (Philadelphia); and (7) the danger of an unconscious spiritual lukewarmness (Laodicea). These dangers the Lord sees, and warns us of, as He walks in the midst of all the churches with all the pastors in His hand.

The Pastor ... "LET HIM HEAR"

Pastors, and all ministers, must be made aware, and kept aware, of the fact that there will be a day of ACCOUNTABILITY. It can be a glorious day of rejoicing in hearing Christ's "Well done" (Matthew 25:21, 23), or a day of "weeping and gnashing of teeth" for the unfaithful servants when they hear Him say, "Depart from me" (Matthew 24:48-51; 25:30, 41).

The temptation may be great to compromise in order to enjoy the popular favor of the majority. The pressure may be strong to preach "smooth things," and to "look the other way," or to "see not" the corruption that calls for rebuke:

"... This is a rebellious people, lying children, children that will not hear the law of the Lord:

"Which say to the seers, See not; and to the prophets, Prophesy not unto us right things, speak unto us smooth things, prophesy deceits" (Isaiah 30:9, 10).

The lure of riches and increased goods may seem like "my opportunity" when it is actually the curse that will cause the Lord to "spue thee out of [His] mouth"!

In order for a church to have the favor of Christ's smile, it may become necessary to sacrifice its **Top-of-the-Top-Ten** "name that thou livest," and take inventory in order to save "the things which remain, that are ready to die."

Seven times the Lord says, "I KNOW THY WORKS." He knows when a pastor is struggling "against the odds," but is patiently, faithfully, uncompromisingly standing for right and truth, and is going through every "open door" to spend and be spent for Christ and His Church.

And He knows "THY SLOTHFULNESS"—"THY UNCONCERN"—"THY NEGLECT"—"THY SELFISH COVETOUSNESS."

"... Woe be to the shepherds of Israel that do feed themselves! should not the shepherds feed the flocks? "Ye eat the fat, and ye clothe you with the wool, ye kill them that are fed: but ye feed not the flock.

"The diseased have ye not strengthened, neither have ye healed that which was sick, neither have ye bound up that which was broken, neither have ye brought again that which was driven away, neither have ye sought that which was lost; but with force and with cruelty have ye ruled them.

"And they were scattered, because there is no shepherd: and they became meat to all the beasts of the field, when they were scattered.

"My sheep wandered through all the mountains, and upon every high hill: yea, my flock was scattered upon all the face of the earth, and none did search or seek after them" (Ezekiel 34: 2-6).

"For the pastors are become brutish, and have not sought the Lord: therefore they shall not prosper, and all their flocks shall be scattered" (Jeremiah 10:21).

Pastor—Church—WHAT IF ... ?

Pastor, what if you and your church should receive a letter from Jesus the Head, in words understandable in the Church's present structure and operation? Would you feel categorized with Smyrna and Philadelphia, with nothing against you? Would you identify more nearly with Pergamos, Thyatira, and Sardis, where physical passion had engulfed them in idolatry (spiritual adultery) and immorality (under the guise of "freedom" and "grace")? Or would you feel more closely associated with Ephesus and Laodicea, where the "first love" had been left behind and a smug self-satisfaction prevailed?

Would the Lord COMMEND you for faithfully preaching the Gospel and making the Church known as the sheltering fold for all of His sheep? for holding fast the doctrine? for suffering persecution rather than compromise the truth? for loving and having the same care one for another? for making the fold so safe for "the ninety and nine" that you could go out in search of the one gone astray? for making every effort and activity contribute something vital to the fulfillment of the real need? Would He assure you of His keeping through "the hour of temptation," and of "the crown of life" in the hereafter?

Or, would He INDICT you and REPROVE you for your unloving, uncaring unconcern for the discouraged and backslidden? for your sympathetic tolerance of questionable doctrine, and satisfying the "itching ears" of those who "will not endure sound doctrine"? for your "liberal" attitude toward worldliness, and your condoning of loose morals? for your personal covetousness, and your irresponsible expenditure of church funds? Would He rebuke the church for allowing a "Jezebel" or a "counterfeit Jew" to continue their teachings and practices unrestrained? for your church roll laden with rebellious and defiantly sinful members? Would He predict the removal of your "candlestick" and threaten to "spue you out"?

We may weep **joyful tears** as we read the Lord's loving words to those pastors and churches which had endured so very much, but had stood true, and were now hearing His promises of good things. And we may shed **tears of sorrow** as we read of those pastors and churches which were such a grief and disappointment to their Master, yet He stood ready to forgive and restore. But we must beware of the "blind spot" with reference to our own failures while the failures of others appear "in living color." Jesus advocated the removal of the "beam" (log) from our own eye before presuming to remove the "mote" (splinter) from our brother's eye (Matthew 7:3-5). Apostle Paul was very specific about unjust judgment:

"Therefore thou art inexcusable, O man, whosoever thou art that judgest: for wherein thou judgest another, thou condemnest thyself; for thou that judgest doest the same things.

"But we are sure that the judgment of God is according to truth against them which commit such things.

"And thinkest thou this, O man, that judgest them which do such things, and doest the same, that thou shalt escape the judgment of God?

"Or despisest thou the riches of his goodness and

forbearance and longsuffering; not knowing that the goodness of God leadeth thee to repentance?

"But after thy hardness and impenitent heart treasurest up unto thyself wrath against the day of wrath and revelation of the righteous judgment of God;

"Who will render to every man according to his deeds" (Romans 2:1-6).

The Hour Is Late!

The book known as "The Revelation of Jesus Christ" was written almost nineteen hundred years ago. The letters to the seven churches have been on record all those years. They have been read by multitudes from every generation since that time. No doubt they have been instrumental in recovering many from their sins and shortcomings. Also, there is little doubt that many have ignored their admonition, and brought upon themselves their own destruction.

We are living too close to the remainder of the "revelation" to take the Lord's admonition lightly. For our own good, and that of the teeming multitudes who must yet be warned, we must make very sure that we do not become so involved in selfish concerns that we leave our Seeking Shepherd standing outside, knocking, and pleading for admission.

A solemn warning given by Him to His inquiring disciples only hours before He wrought our eternal salvation, and purchased the Church of God with His own blood, seems a proper conclusion for this course.

> "And he spake to them a parable; Behold the fig tree, and all the trees;
>
> "When they now shoot forth, ye see and know of your own selves that summer is now nigh at hand.
>
> "So likewise ye, when ye see these things come to pass, know ye that the kingdom of God is nigh at hand.
>
> "Verily I say unto you, This generation shall not pass away, till all be fulfilled.
>
> "Heaven and earth shall pass away: but my words shall not pass away.
>
> "And take heed to yourselves, lest at any time your hearts be overcharged with surfeiting, and drunkenness, and cares of this life, and so that day come upon you unawares.

"For as a snare shall it come on all them that dwell on the face of the whole earth.

"Watch ye therefore, and pray always, that ye may be accounted worthy to escape all these things that shall come to pass, and to stand before the Son of man" (Luke 21:29-36).

"AMEN. EVEN SO, COME, LORD JESUS."

THE SEVEN CHURCHES OF ASIA

EXAMINATION

1. List the seven churches of Asia in the order addressed in Revelation, chapters 2 and 3:
   1. _____   5. _____
   2. _____   6. _____
   3. _____   7. _____
   4. _____

2. Write True (T) or False (F) before each statement:
   [ ] (a) The entire Book of Revelation is addressed to the churches.
   [ ] (b) The "revelation" has no relevance to the Church in our day.
   [ ] (c) The "seven Spirits of God" means that each of the seven churches had a separate Spirit of God.

3. Fill the blanks from the list of words following each statement:
   (a) The early presentation of these letters seems an admonition to the churches and pastors to consider their _____ and _____ in the light of future end-results.
   (importance   accountability   capability   responsibility)
   (b) The sword of the Spirit is _____.
   (the Holy Ghost   the wrath of God   the Word of God   speaking in tongues)
   (c) True repentance is _____ and _____.
   (saying, "I'm sorry"   resolving to do better   godly sorrow   turning from sin)

4. Write in the correct words in these verses of Scripture:
   (a) "For not he that _____ himself is approved, but whom the _____ commendeth" (2 Corinthians 10:18).
   (reproveth   world   church   commendeth   helpeth   Word   Lord)
   (b) "For the things which are seen are _____ ; but the things which are not seen are _____," (2 Corinthians 4:18).

145

(certain visible eternal temporal tempting invisible)
(c) "... Whosoever therefore will be a friend of the _____ is the _____ of God" (James 4:4).
(world friend church son enemy Jew chosen)

5. Put an X before each statement that applies:
The disciplinary process for dealing with wrongdoers has the following objectives:
[ ] (a) the exercise of authority
[ ] (b) the purity of the Church
[ ] (c) the glory of God
[ ] (d) the punishment of the wrongdoer
[ ] (e) the spiritual good of the member being disciplined

6. Fill the blanks with the correct words:
(a) Apokalypsis is the Greek word for _____.
(b) The golden candlesticks were the _____.
(c) The seven stars were the _____.

7. Write True (T) or False (F) before each statement:
[ ] (a) The Nicolaitanes' "hateful deeds" were their licentious lives and impure doctrines.
[ ] (b) The doctrine of Balaam taught the people to commit fornication.
[ ] (c) Unrestricted "freedom" is actually a deadly form of bondage.
[ ] (d) Overcomers already "have their reward" in this world.

8. Fill the blanks from the lists of words following each statement:
(a) _____ is spiritual adultery.
(fornication unfaithfulness idolatry)
(b) _____ is like a blend of devotion and apathy.
(Balaamism Jezebelism heresy lukewarmness orthodoxy)
(c) Egotism is _____.
(spiritual blindness spiritual coldness self-exaltation love of money)

9. Put an X before each statement that applies:

Some possible causes of spiritual lukewarmness include:
[ ] (a) A church membership syndrome
[ ] (b) Being either "hot" or "cold" in service for God
[ ] (c) Love for the things of the world
[ ] (d) An education obsession
[ ] (e) Wealth

10. Write in the correct words in these verses of Scripture:
    (a) "And ye shall know the _____, and the _____ shall make you free" (John 8:32).
    (b) "Wherefore come out from among them, and be ye _____, saith the Lord, and _____ the unclean thing; and I will _____ you" (2 Corinthians 6:17).
    (c) "Think not that I am come to send _____ on earth: I came not to send _____, but a sword" (Matthew 10:34).

11. Write Yes (Y) or No (N) before each question:
    [ ] (a) Was Christ created?
    [ ] (b) Did A. J. Tomlinson teach that the "falling away" of 2 Thessalonians 2:3 began with the Nicean Council in A.D. 325?
    [ ] (c) Is the "religious conglomerate" of our day the Church of the living God?
    [ ] (d) Is it possible to labor "in Christ's name" without a love He can accept?
    [ ] (e) Can any ordained minister be made an apostle?

12. Put an X before the possible causes of Sardis' "dead" or "dying condition."
    [ ] (a) empty professions of faith
    [ ] (b) external pride
    [ ] (c) "at ease in Zion"
    [ ] (d) compromised truth
    [ ] (e) not enough social activity

13. Write True (T) or False (F) before each statement:
    [ ] (a) Reformation and new resolve constitute repentance.
    [ ] (b) When truth is compromised, sound doctrine is often given a less restricted meaning.

[ ] (c) Through traditional worship and works, a mere "form" may come to be thought of as "the power."
[ ] (d) If spiritual experiences are not genuine, the empty professions are deadly deceptive.
[ ] (e) By belief in Christ's perfect work for us, our good works are "counted for righteousness."

14. Fill the blanks with the proper words:
    (a) King _____ did more to provoke the Lord God of Israel to anger than all the kings of Israel that were before him.
    (b) Men may cause us to fail in faith so that we will forfeit the _____ we have hoped to obtain.
    (c) _____ would not be deception if it were easily apparent.
    (d) Christ will confess the overcomer's name before His _____ and His _____.
    (e) Revelation 12:5, tells us that Christ shall rule with a _____ _____.

15. Write in the correct words in these verses of Scripture:
    (a) "Nevertheless I have somewhat against thee, because thou hast left thy _____ _____ " (Revelation 2:4).
    (b) "... He that overcometh shall not be hurt of the _____ _____ " (Revelation 2:11).
    (c) "... I know thy works, that thou hast a name that thou _____, and art _____ " (Revelation 3:1).
    (d) "As many as I love, I _____ and _____: be zealous therefore, and repent" (Revelation 3:19).
    (e) "He that hath an _____, let him _____ what the _____ saith unto the churches" (Revelation 3:13).

16. Fill the blanks from the list of words following each statement:
    (a) The Laodicean's "nakedness" represented their _____ _____. (sinful state   poverty   brazenness   pride)
    (b) A church that has learned to "sin and shout" is _____ _____ _____ God.
    (a friend of   a lover of   an enemy of   a true witness for)

148

(c) A preoccupation with doctrine can result in a _____ spirit with little love and grace.
(worldly   victorious   deceptive   legalistic)
(d) Jesus warned that through _____ _____ _____ _____ "... If it were possible, (false christs and false prophets) shall deceive the very elect."
(words of great wisdom   works of great evil   great signs and wonders   great promises of record)
(e) For man looketh on the _____ appearance but the Lord looketh on the _____.
(inward   soul   outward   heart)

17. Put an X before each statement that applies:
The "first works" might include:
[ ] (a) confession
[ ] (b) preaching
[ ] (c) water baptism
[ ] (d) restitution
[ ] (e) reformation

18. Write True (T) or False (F) before each statement:
[ ] (a) The angels are generally considered to be the pastors of the churches.
[ ] (b) John received the revelation of Jesus Christ on the isle called Patmos.
[ ] (c) Cowardice in preaching the truth leads to compromise and deception.
[ ] (d) The stumblingblock characteristic of the doctrine of Balaam was its "religious" characteristic.
[ ] (e) The term "dogs" was a term of reproach.

19. Underline the proper words in each parentheses to make the statement correct:
(a) "The wages of unrighteousness" refer to Balaam's (covetousness   persistence   blessing of Israel).
(b) "Peace at any price" is (God-like   compromise   perfection).
(c) The doctrine of the Nicolaitanes was a (love for the world   commitment to Christ   life of holiness).
(d) Egotism is related to (spirituality   secular humanism   blind confidence).
(e) The modern name for Smyrna is (Izmir   Cairo   Durban   Athens)

20. Match by putting the number from the second column before the proper words in the first column:

[ ] (a) Charity   1. represents authority and power
[ ] (b) Keys   2. easily cheated or tricked
[ ] (c) Antinomianism   3. the deceiver's way of gaining a following
[ ] (d) Gullibility   4. "believe God and do as you please" philosophy
[ ] (e) Counterfeit   5. love in action

NAME _____

ADDRESS _____

_____